What NOT to Say!

What NOT to Say!

Produced by Cliff Road Books

Printed in The United States of America

ISBN: 1-58173-360-7

This work is a compilation from numerous sources. Every effort has been made to ensure accuracy. However, the publisher cannot be responsible for incorrect information. Definitions are from the *Merriam Webster Dictionary*, 10th edition.

Order online at www.booksamillion.com

What NOT to Say!

Compiled and Edited by
Linda J. Beam

About the Author

Linda J. Beam holds a B.A. in English from Judson College, and an M.A. in English from the University of Alabama at Birmingham. Her extensive editorial experience includes work with medical journals and textbooks, and a variety of corporate publications. In addition, she has developed and presented business communication seminars on business writing, and basic grammar and punctuation. She currently works as Managing Editor at Crane Hill Publishers in Birmingham, Alabama.

Contents

Introduction

In our work and in our everyday lives, all of us communicate with other people. Whether in casual conversations or in formal presentations, the words we use tell who we are and what we know. We need only to recall Dan Quayle's infamous "p-o-t-a-t-o-e" to realize how choosing, or spelling, words incorrectly can undermine a professional image. Simply put, when we are called on to speak, we need to know the correct words to use and how to present our thoughts concisely.

The written word is equally important. Yet many people find writing to be one of the most difficult tasks they face. They believe or think they are not prepared to do it, they spend too much time on it, and find that their results are not completely satisfying. It is no wonder they face writing with dread and procrastination. Despite this, speaking and writing well are important skills that can bring visibility in many aspects of life.

This book will offer help with some of the finer points of language that can make such a difference when we try to convey our thoughts and ideas. To help with correct pronunciation of words for speakers, there are tips designated as "Commonly Mispronounced Words." Speakers and writers alike will find helpful the extensive section on "Commonly Confused Words," as well as the smaller section on "Commonly Misused Words and Phrases." For quick reference, there are lists of "Commonly Misspelled Words," and "Redundancies." To help fine-tune grammar glitches, there is a listing of what I believe to be the "Top 10 Mistakes, Abuses, and Misuses" in dealing with written and spoken language.

Finally, interspersed alongside the text are humorous quotes to remind us that language missteps are no respecter of person. These challenge us to not be guilty of the same mistakes, and encourage us by offering proof that we are not alone in our struggle to express ourselves precisely.

Linda J. Beam

Commonly Mispronounced Words

Commonly Mispronounced Words

Some words are chronically mispronounced. Here are some guidelines to help you get them right.

Absorption (ab-SORP-shun) NOT: ab-SORB-shun.
Accessory (ak-SESS-se-ree) NOT: ah-SESS-ry. There's an "ack" sound at the beginning of this word, though some mispronounce it as if the two "Cs" were to be sounded the same as the two "Ss."
Accidentally (ax-sa-DEN-ta-lee) NOT: ax-a-dent-lee.
Across (ah-KROS) NOT: Acrost, acrossed. The man across the street from me is waiting for the light to turn. The man crossed the street after the light turned.
Adultery (a-DULL-ter-ee) NOT: a-DULL- tree.

> **"Sometimes you can observe a lot by watching."**
> Yogi Berra

Affidavit (aff-a-DAY-vit) NOT: affa-DAY-vid.
Aggravate (AGG-rah-vate) NOT: agger-vate.
Amandine (a-man-DEEN) NOT: al-mon-DEEN. Even though amandine means prepared or served with almonds, almond is not the root word.
Alzheimer's Disease (ALTS-hi-mers) NOT: Old-timers, al-timers.
Anyway NOT: Anyways. As in "So, anyways, we were at the mall, and..." There is only one, so please leave off the "s."
Archipelago (ar-ki-PEL-a-go) NOT: arch-i-PEL-a-go.
Arctic (ARC-tic) NOT: AR-tic. There are two "Cs" in arctic, and they should both be pronounced. However, some dictionaries have begun to use "Ar-tic" as an acceptable alternative pronunciation.

Commonly Mispronounced Words

Arkansas (AR-kan-saw) NOT: AR-kan-sas. The latter pronunciation is only correct when referring to the river, not the state (even though some locals pronounce it that way).
Ask (ASK) NOT: AKS (the incorrect pronunciation sounds like axe).
Asterisk: (AS-ter-isk) NOT: AS-ter-ik. That second "s" is not silent.
Athlete (ATH-leet) NOT: ATH-a-leet. There is no "a" after "th."

Barbed wire NOT: Bob wire. This is wire that is twisted and barbed, thus the name barbed wire. As far as I know this wasn't invented by someone named Bob.
Boise (BOI-zi) NOT: BOI-si or BOI-z, although some locals use BOI-si.
Business (BIZ-niss) NOT: BID-niss. I think this started out as slang that later became a common pronunciation.

Candidate (CAN-di-date) NOT: cannidate. Remember that first "d."
Camera (KAM-rah) NOT: kam-rie.
Cardsharp NOT: cardshark. The card player is sharp, not a shark.
Caribbean (ka-ra-BEE-an) NOT: Ka-RIB-ee-an. Although most dictionaries list both as acceptable, the Ka-ra-BEE-an is most commonly accepted as correct. Some people think that Ka-ra-BEE-an is correct when used as a noun: "When I retire I'm moving to the Caribbean," and Ka-RIB-ee-an when used as an adjective: "the Caribbean islands." Dictionaries, however, do not offer this difference.
Celtic (KEL-tic) NOT: SEL-tic. Unless you're referring to the Boston Celtics, KEL-tic is the correct pronunciation.

Chaise Longue (SHAZE long). This literally means "long chair." Many speakers confuse French longue with English "lounge," resulting in the mispronunciation "chase lounge."
Chest of Drawers NOT: Chester drawers. This is a very common mispronunciation in the South, but is also used in other parts of the country.
Chimera (kiy-MEER-a) NOT: CHIM-er-a.
Chimney (CHIM-knee) NOT: CHIM-ley.
Comfortable (COM-fort-a-ble or COMF-ta-ble) NOT: COMF-ter-ble.

Dilate (DIE-late) NOT: DIE-ah-late. There is only one "a."
Diphtheria (dif-THEER-e-a) NOT: dip-THEER-e-a. The "ph" is pronounced "f."
Disastrous (di-ZAS-trus) NOT: di-ZAS-ter-es. This is three syllables, not four.
Drown NOT: drowned or drownded. The "ed" is added only to the past tense. "Don't let your dog drown in the lake." "My dog drowned in the lake last year."
Duct Tape NOT: Duck Tape. Although there is a brand that manufactures duct tape named Duck Tape, the generic word to describe silver tape that is used to tape air ducts is duct tape.

Ecstatic (eck-STA-tic) NOT: es-STA-tic.
Electoral (eh-LEK-tor-al) NOT: eh-lek-TOR-al. Remember that the root is eh-LEKT.
Erudition (ayr-yoo-DISH-en) NOT: ayr-a-DISH-en.
Especially (is-PE-shel-le) NOT: Expecially. It's ess, not ex.

Espresso (ess-PRESS-oh) NOT: ex-PRESS-oh. Again, it's ess, not ex.
Etcetera (et-SE-te-ra) NOT: ek-SE-te-ra.
Excerpt (EX-serpt) NOT: EX-cerp. Remember the "t."

February (FEB-roo-aree) NOT: FEB-yoo-aree.
Fictional (FIK-shen-al) NOT: fic-TI-shen-al. The latter is a combination of fictitious and fictional. Choose one of the real words.
Figure (FIG-yer) NOT: FIG-er.
Foliage (FO-li-ij) NOT: FOI-lij or FO-lij. While some dictionaries list the other two pronunciations as acceptable, most well-educated people don't agree.

> **"The President has kept all the promises he intended to keep."**
>
> George Stephanopolous, former Clinton aide

Folk (FOK) NOT: FOLK. The "l" is silent.
Forte (FORT) NOT: for-TAY. This is a common mispronunciation, but most people understand that it means something at which someone excels.

Government (GUH-vern-ment) NOT: GUH-ver-ment. Be sure to pronounce the "n."
Greenwich Village (GRE-nij) NOT: Green-witch. Most people in New York just say "the village."
Grievous (GREV-us) NOT: GREV-e-us.

Harass (Ha-RASS) NOT: HAR-ass. While both of these are considered correct, the preferred pronunciation is Ha-RASS; the other pronunciation sounds pretentious.
Hawaii (he-WA-yee) NOT: Hu-WA-e or Hu-VA-ee.

> **"Live within your income, even if you have to borrow to do so."**
>
> Josh Billings

Height (HITE) NOT: HITHE. This word ends in "t," not "th."
Hors d'oeuvres (or-DERVES).These are any variety of foods served as appetizers.
Houston This is a much-debated one. The street in New York City is pronounced HOUS-ton. The city in Texas is "officially" pronounced HUE-ston, but most Texans will tell you it's EWE-ston (the "h" is silent).

Impotent (IM-po-tent) NOT: Im-PO-tent.
Inaugural (in-NAWG-yoor-al) NOT: in-NAWG-a-ral.
Illinois (Ill-a-NOY) NOT: I-la-NOIZ. The "s" is silent.
Insouciant (in-SOO-see-ant) NOT: in-SOO-shant.
Interesting (IN-tres-ting) NOT: IN-te-res-ting. The second syllable is normally silent in "interesting." It's nonstandard to go out of your way to pronounce the "ter," and definitely substandard to say "innaresting."

Jewelry (JEW-el-re) NOT: JEWL-er-y. To remember the standard pronunciation, just say "jewel" and add "-ree" on the end. The British spelling is much fancier: "jewellery."

Kindergarten (KIN-der-gar-tin) NOT: kinney garden. This incorrect pronunciation probably originated with a kindergartener.

Lambaste (lam-BASTE) NOT: lam-BAST.
Laissez-faire (LAZ-ay-fair) NOT: lazy-fare. This means "let it be," or more precisely, "the economic doctrine of avoiding state regulation of the economy."
Larvae (LAR-vah) NOT: LAR-vay.
Library (LIBE-rare-ee) NOT: LIBE-air-ee.
Louisville (LOO-i-vil) NOT: LOO-is-vil or LOO-vil.

M

Mackinac (MAK-a-naw) NOT: MAK-a-nack. The last syllable of this island north of Michigan rhymes with "saw."
Mauve (MOHVE; rhymes with "grove") NOT: MAWV.
Mayonnaise (MAY-a-naze) NOT: MAN-aze.
Melbourne (MEL-burn) NOT: MEL-born.
Menstruation (men-STROO-a-shun) NOT: men-STRAY-shun.
Miniature (MI-nee-a-ture) NOT: MIN-a-ture.

Minuscule (MIN-uh-skyool) NOT: MIN-ih-skyool.
Mischievous (MISS-che-vus) NOT: mis-CHEE-vee-us.
Mispronunciation (mis-pro-nun-see-A-shun) NOT: mis-pro-nown-see-A-shun.
Missouri (Mi-ZUR-ee) NOT: Mi-ZUR-a. Some locals of Missouri say "Mi-ZUR-a."
Moray (MUR-ee) NOT: More-AY. Region in Scotland. Correct pronunciation rhymes with hurry.

Neither (NEE-ther or NI-ther) Although NEE-ther is preferred in most dictionaries, both are correct.
Nevada (Nuh-VAH-duh) This is a little closer to the original Spanish pronunciation than the way Nevadans pronounce the name of their home state, but the correct middle syllable is the same "a" sound as in "sad." When East Coast broadcasters use the first pronunciation, they mark themselves as outsiders.
Nuclear (NUKE-lee-ar) NOT: NUKE-yoo-lar.
Nuptial (NUP-shul) NOT: NUP-shoo-al.

Often (OFF-en) NOT: Off-ten. The "t" is silent.
Once (WUNCE) NOT: WUNCED. This is more common in certain regions, but is never correct.
Oregon (OR-e-gun) NOT: ORE-e-gone.
Orient (OR-e-ent) NOT: OR-e-n-tate. This is only a three-syllable word.
Ought (aught, as in taught) NOT: orte. There is no "r" in ought.

Pecan (PA-con) NOT: PEE-can. Any true Southerner (and Webster) knows that the preferred pronunciation is PA-con.
Percolate (PERC-o-late) NOT: PERC-u-late.
Peremptory (per-EMP-tor-ee) NOT: PRE-emp-tor-ee.
Picture (PIK-cher) NOT: pit-cher.
Plenitude (PLEN-i-tude) NOT: PLENT-i-tude.
Preferably (PREFF-er-ub-lee). This is the standard pronunciation, with the first syllable stressed, just like in "preference." U.S. dictionaries now recognize the pronunciation with the first two syllables as in "prefer," but this sounds awkward to some people.

> **"Always be sincere, even when you don't mean it."**
> Irene Parker

Prerogative (pre-ROG-a-tive) NOT: per-ROG-a-tive.
Prescription (pre-SKRIP-shun) NOT: per-SKRIP-shun.
Probably (PROB-ab-ly) NOT: PRAH-bal-ly, PROB-ly.
Pronunciation (pro-NUN-see-A-shun) NOT: pro-NOUN-see-A-shun.
Prostate (PROS-tate) NOT: PROS-trate. Prostate is the name of a male gland. There is no "r" after the "t." There is, however, another legitimate word, "prostrate," which means to lie face down in a spirit of humility.
Pumpkin (PUMP-kin) NOT: Punkin. It's an "m," not an "n." Some dictionaries offer "pungkin" or "punkin" as accepted pronunciations, but I recommend sticking with the pronunciation that won't have people wondering if you mispronounced the word.

Q

Quebec Depending on where you're from it's either Que-BEC, KI-bec, or KA-bec. Webster's says it's KWI-bec.

Racism (RAY-cizm) The "c" in racism and "racist" is pronounced as a simple "s" sound. Don't confuse it with the "sh" sound in "racial."

> **"They misunderestimated me."**
>
> President George W. Bush

Realtor (REEL-tor) NOT: REE-la-tor. There is no "a" after the "l."
Recognize (RECK-ug-nize) NOT: RECK-uh-nize. Sound the "g."
Recur (ri-KUR) NOT: re-o-KUR.
Relevant (REL-e-vant) NOT: REV-e-lant. The "v" should be pronounced with the third syllable.
Respite (RES-pit) NOT: RE-spite.
Rinse (RINS) NOT: RINSH that rhymes with wrench. There is no "h" at the end of this.

Salmon (SA-mon) NOT: SAL-mon. The "l" is silent.
Sherbet (SHER-bet) NOT: SHER-bert. There is only one "r."
Spurious (SPYUR-ee-us) NOT: SPUR-ee-us. The correct pronunciation rhymes with furious.
Supposedly (sup-POSE-ed-ly) NOT: sup-POSE-ab-ly.

T

Taut (taut) NOT: taunt.
Tentative (TEN-ta-tive) NOT: TEN-na-tive. Sound all three "Ts."
Tenterhooks (TEN-ter-hooks) NOT: tenderhooks.
Ticklish (TIK-lish) NOT: TIK-i-lish.
Toward (TO-ward) NOT: (TOR-ward).
Triathlon (try-ATH-lon) NOT: try-ATH-a-lon. There is only one "a."
Twice (twise) NOT: twiced. Like once/onced, this is more common in some regions than others.

Uranus (YUR-ay-nus) NOT: Yur-A-nus. Some people use the incorrect pronunciation because the correct one sounds a little vulgar.

Verbiage (VER-be-ij) NOT: VER-bij.

Wash (Wah-sh) NOT: warsh. The latter is common, but incorrect. This is carried even further by some inhabitants of Washington, D.C., where the pronunciation "Warshington" is common, but still incorrect.

Worcester (WUS-ter) NOT: WAR-cess-ter or WAR-chest-er. This is a town in Massachusetts, a town in England, and also the brand name of a sauce. They are all pronounced the same way. However, residents of the two towns sometimes drop the last "r" as well: "WUS-ta."

Zoology (ZO-ol-o-gy) NOT: ZOO-ah-lo-gy.

Commonly Confused Words

Commonly Confused Words

We all have certain words and phrases that we confuse with other similar ones. In a few instances, the difference in their meanings may be so subtle as to make them interchangeable. But with others, their misuse is more glaring. Here are some that are often used incorrectly.

Abbreviations / Acronyms

An example of an *abbreviation* is CIA (for Central Intelligence Agency), because the letters"C," "I," and "A" do not form the word "See-a." An *acronym* is a word that is formed by the first letter or letters of each word in a multi-word name. Some common acronyms are:

MASH: Mobile Army Surgical Hospital
SCUBA: Self-Contained Underwater Breathing Apparatus
RADAR: Radio Detecting and Ranging

Abjure / Adjure

Abjure means to renounce or reject. *Adjure* means to command solemnly or strongly advise.

Accept / Except

To *accept* is to receive something willingly. *Except* means with the exclusion of.

Adopted / Adoptive

Adopted and *adoptive* both mean "acquired through adoption," but they are not synonyms. Adopted is the past tense of the verb adopt. "My sister adopted a child." *Adoptive* is an adjective. "My sister is an adoptive parent."

Commonly Confused Words

Adverse / Averse

Adverse means opposed to or acting against. "The medication I took had an adverse reaction. It made me feel worse, not better." *Averse* means actively against. It is the root word of aversion. "Cautious investors are often averse to taking risks."

Affect / Effect

Affect means to bring about change. "I plan to affect my sister's decision by giving her propaganda." *Effect* is the result of another action. "The sound of the ocean has a calming effect on my nerves."

> **"When large numbers of men are unable to find work, unemployment results."**
>
> Former President Calvin Coolidge

Affluence / Effluence

Affluence is wealth. *Effluence* is an act or an instance of something flowing out.

Alliterate / Illiterate

Words with the same initial sound *alliterate,* like "wild and wooly." People who can't read are *illiterate*.

All ready / Already

All ready refers to all people or things being prepared. "We were all ready to leave at 9:00." *Already* refers to time. "The movie had already started when we arrived."

All right / Alright

Alright is informal, and is considered non-standard English. I recommend avoiding it.

Commonly Confused Words

All together / Altogether

All together is used when referring to a group of people or things being in one place. "My family was all together last Thanksgiving." *Altogether* is used to mean entirely: "I am not altogether decided about where I'm going on my next vacation."

> **"When I want your opinion, I'll give it to you."**
>
> Samuel Goldwyn

Allude / Refer

Allude means to refer to something indirectly. *Refer* means to mention something directly by naming it.

Allusion / Illusion

An *allusion* is an indirect reference (root word: allude). *Illusion* is a noun that means a misconception or misleading image.

Alot / A lot

Perhaps this common spelling error began because there does exist in English a word spelled "allot" which is a verb meaning to apportion or grant. The correct form, with *a* and *lot* separated by a space, is not often encountered because formal writers usually use other expressions such as "a great deal, " "often," etc. If you can't remember the rule, just remind yourself that just as you wouldn't write *alittle*, you shouldn't write *alot*.

Altar / Alter

An *altar* is a table or similar object used for sacred purposes. *Alter* is a verb meaning to change.

AM / PM

AM comes from the Latin phrase "Ante Meridiem," meaning "before noon" and PM comes from "Post Meridiem," meaning "after noon." Therefore noon is not 12:00 PM, it's just noon. The same goes for midnight.

Commonly Confused Words

Ambiguous / Ambivalent
Both of these are legitimate words. *Ambiguous* means obscure, doubtful, or uncertain. *Ambivalent* is uncertainty or indecisiveness.

Among / Amongst
While *amongst* is not considered incorrect, *among* is much more common, and sounds much less awkward and old-fashioned to most ears.

Amount / Number
Use the word *amount* to refer to quantities that are measured in bulk; use *number* to refer to things that can actually be counted. "I don't know the total amount of paper we need, but I know a number of people in the office need it."

Anecdote / Antidote
An *anecdote* is "a usually short narrative of an interesting, amusing, or biographical incident." An *antidote* is "something that relieves or counteracts," usually when referring to the effects of poison.

Angel / Angle
An *angel* is a spiritual being with wings associated with heaven; an *angle* is a corner where two lines meet or a point of view.

Anxious / Eager
Anxious means worried or feeling uneasy about something in the future. *Eager* means expectancy or impatient desire or interest. Anxious has a bad connotation, while eager has a good connotation. "I am anxious about getting my tooth pulled, but eager to go on vacation the next week."

Commonly Confused Words

Appraise / Apprise

Appraise means to put a value on something. "The jeweler will appraise the bracelet." *Apprise* means to inform someone. "Please apprise me of the jeweler's decision."

As if / Like

As if is generally preferred in formal writing over *like* in sentences such as "The conductor looks as if he's ready to begin the symphony." But in colloquial speech, *like* prevails: "He spends money like it's going out of style."

Assure / Ensure / Insure

To *assure* a person of something is to make him or her confident of it. According to Associated Press style, to *ensure* that something happens is to make certain that it does, and to *insure* is to issue an insurance policy. Other authorities, however, consider *ensure* and *insure* interchangeable.

Atheist / A theist

These words are the opposite of each other. An *atheist* is one who disbelieves or denies the existence of God. A *theist* is one who believes in the existence of God.

Augur / Auger

An *augur* was an ancient Roman prophet, and as a verb the word means "foretell": "Their love augurs well for a successful marriage." Don't mix this word up with *auger*, a tool for boring holes. Some people mishear the phrase "augurs well" as "all goes well" and mistakenly use that instead.

Avocation / Vocation

Your *avocation* is just your hobby; don't mix it up with your job, your *vocation*.

Commonly Confused Words

Backslash / Slash
This is a *slash*: /. Because the top of it leans forward, it is sometimes called a "forward slash." This is a *backslash*: \. Notice the way it leans back, distinguishing it from the regular slash. Web addresses never contain backslashes. Newer browsers will silently correct this error, but older ones may not.

Bazaar / Bizarre
A *bazaar* is a market where goods are sold. *Bizarre* is an adjective meaning "strange," "weird."

> **"Republicans understand the importance of bondage between a mother and child."**
>
> Former Vice President Dan Quayle

Bemuse / Amuse
When you *bemuse* someone, you confuse them, and not necessarily in an entertaining way. Don't confuse this word with *amuse*, which means to occupy in a pleasant manner.

Beside / Besides
Beside is a preposition that means next to: "My dog is standing beside my cat." *Besides* is an adverb that means also: "Besides being sweet, my cat is the most beautiful cat that ever lived."

Between / Among
Between indicates a relationship involving two people or things. "Our conversation was just between the two of us." *Among* indicates a group of three or more. "We discussed the problem among the department managers."

Commonly Confused Words

Bias / Biased

A person who is influenced by a *bias* is *biased*. The expression is not "They're bias," but "They're biased." Also, many people say someone is "biased toward" something or someone when they mean biased against. To have a bias toward something is to be biased in its favor.

> **"I marvel at the strength of human weakness."**
>
> Irish folklore

Bimonthly / Semimonthly

While *bimonthly* can mean every two months or twice a month, its most common use is to mean every two months. *Semimonthly* strictly means twice a month.

Borrow / Loan

In some dialects it is common to substitute *borrow* for *loan* or *lend*, as in "Borrow me that hammer of yours, will you, Jeb?" In standard English the person providing an item can loan it, but the person receiving it borrows it.

Both / Each

There are times when it is important to use *each* instead of *both*. Few people will be confused if you say "I gave both of the boys a baseball glove," meaning that you gave them one each. But you risk confusion if you say "I gave both of the boys $50." It is possible to construe this sentence as meaning that the boys shared the same $50 gift. "I gave each of the boys $50" is clearer.

Breach / Breech

A *breach* is something broken off or open, as in a breach in a military line during combat. *Breech* however, refers to rear ends, as in "breeches" (slang spelling "britches"). Thus "breech cloth," "breech birth," or "breech-loading gun."

Commonly Confused Words

Bring / Take

To determine which to use, ask where the action is headed. If it's toward you, use *bring*. If it's away from you use *take*. "Please bring me the report after you take the mail to the mailroom."

Capital / Capitol

While *capital* has several meanings, like accumulation of wealth or the size of a letter, the confusion comes in when referencing a city or town that is the seat of government. In this case, the city or town itself is the *capital*; the building in which the legislative assembly meets is the *capitol*. The word *capital* can also be used to refer to a city that excels in some activity, as in "the fashion capital of the world."

Caramel / Carmel

Unless you're referring to the city in California, *caramel* is the word you're looking for. *Caramel* is a candy or topping made by melting and browning sugar.

Cavalry / Calvary

Cavalry is an army component mounted on horseback. *Calvary* is the hill near Jerusalem where Jesus was crucified.

Celibate / Chaste

You can be celibate without being chaste, and chaste without being celibate. A *celibate* person is one who abstains from sexual intercourse, usually by reason of religious vows. *Chaste* means to be morally pure in thought or conduct.

Cement / Concrete

A lot of people say *cement* when they really mean *concrete*. *Cement* is merely an ingredient of concrete, and is a general term for a particular type of glue. It can also be any agent that holds objects or people together. "Love is the cement that holds the world together." *Concrete* is a hard substance made by mixing cementing material and sand or rock. The hard, white material that most sidewalks, driveways, and patios are made of is concrete.

Chicano / Hispanic / Latino

Chicano means "Mexican-American;" *Hispanic* includes people with a Spanish as well as a Latin-American heritage; and *Latino* means Latin-American.

Cite / Site

Cite is a verb that means to quote as an authority or as proof. "My doctor cited a study in a medical journal when telling me his recommended course of treatment." *Site* is a noun meaning location. "The building site of our new school is beautiful."

Click / Clique

Click means "to strike, move, or produce with a click" or "to fit together: hit it off." The latter meaning may be why this word is often misused in place of *clique,* which means "a narrow exclusive circle or group of persons." "A *clique* of friends usually all *click*."

Collaborate / Corroborate

People who work together on a project *collaborate* (share their labor); people who support your testimony as a witness *corroborate* (strengthen by confirming) it.

Commonly Confused Words

Colons / Semicolons

These punctuation marks are often confused. A detailed explanation may be found later in the book in a section entitled "Special Usage and Style Problems."

Compare / Contrast

Compare means "to examine the character or qualities of especially in order to discover similarities or differences." Since this definition already includes differences, there's no need to add *and contrast*. To do so would be redundant.

> **"Moving from Wales to Italy is like moving to a different country."**
>
> Ian Rush

Complement / Compliment / Complimentary

Complement may be a noun or a verb; it means to complete (verb), or something that completes (noun). "I bought the shoes to complement the suit." A *compliment* is an expression of praise or admiration. You can compliment someone for a job well done (verb), or you can receive a compliment about your new haircut (noun). "Mom gave me a compliment on the job I did." Something that is free (refreshments, upgrade in class on a plane) is *complimentary*. This refers to the phrase "with our compliments."

Comprise / Compose

Comprise means to include or to be made up of; *compose* means to make up or to form. According to the traditional rule, "The whole comprises the parts, and the parts compose the whole."

Commonly Confused Words

Comptroller / Controller

Both of these words mean the same thing, and should both be pronounced "controller." Because more and more people pronounce *comptroller* just as it is spelled instead of *controller*, the former has become accepted by *Webster's*. However, *controller* is still the preferred pronunciation and spelling, so it's better to stick with that. *The Oxford English Dictionary* considers "comptroller" to have begun as a misspelling of "controller."

Concurrent / Consecutive

Concurrent means happening at the same time. *Consecutive* means following one after the other.

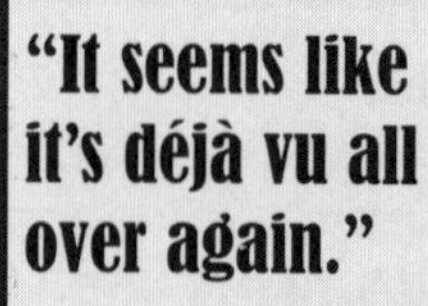

"It seems like it's déjà vu all over again."
Yogi Berra

Connote / Denote

Connote is a verb that means to be associated with or to imply. "Screaming connotes fear." *Denote* is a verb that means to make known, announce, or to refer to specifically, as opposed to just implying.

Continual / Continuous

Continuous refers to actions that are uninterrupted: "My upstairs neighbor played his stereo continuously from 6:00 PM to 3:30 AM." *Continual* actions, however, need not be uninterrupted, only repeated. "My father continually urges me to get a job."

Conversate / Converse

Conversate is what is called a "back-formation" based on the noun "conversation." But the verb for this sort of thing is *converse*.

Commonly Confused Words

Convince / Persuade

Convince means to prove something to someone without doubt – one generally convinces someone of something. *Persuade* means to push someone over the line, usually someone who was "on the fence." *Persuade* is usually used in terms of persuading a person to do something. In other words, one *convinces* a person that something is true but *persuades* a person to do something. Generally speaking, convincing usually requires more effort than persuading.

Core / Corps

Apples have *cores*. A *corps* is an organization, like the Peace Corps. They are both pronounced the same way: core.

Council / Counsel

A *council* is a noun meaning an assembly called together for discussion or deliberation. *Counsel* is a noun meaning advice or guidance. It is also a verb meaning to give advice or guidance. A *councilor* is a person sitting on a council, and a *counselor* is one who is giving counsel.

Credible / Credulous

Credible means "believable" or "trustworthy." It is also used in a more abstract sense, meaning "worthy." *Credulous*, a much rarer word, means "gullible." See also "incredulous/incredible."

Crescendo / Climax

When something is growing louder or more intense, it is going through a *crescendo* (from an Italian word meaning "growing"). A crescendo of cheers by an enthusiastic audience grows until it reaches a *climax*, or peak.

Commonly Confused Words

Criterion / Criteria

Criterion is a standard by which something is judged. *Criteria* is the plural form. You can have one criterion or many criteria.

Critique / Criticize

A *critique* is a detailed evaluation of something. The formal way to request one is "Give me your critique," though people often say informally "Critique this," meaning "Evaluate it thoroughly." But *critique* as a verb is not synonymous with *criticize* and should not be routinely substituted for it.

Current / Currant

Current is an adjective having to do with the present time, and can also be a noun naming a thing that, like time, flows: electrical current, currents of public opinion. *Currant* refers only to little fruits.

> **"Wagner's music is better than it sounds."**
>
> Mark Twain

Damped / Dampened

When the vibration of a wheel is reduced it is *damped*, but when you drive through a puddle your tire is *dampened. Dampened* always has to do with wetting, if only metaphorically: "The announcement that Bob's parents were staying home after all dampened the spirits of the party-goers." The parents are being a wet blanket.

Defuse / Diffuse

You *defuse* a dangerous situation by treating it like a bomb and removing its fuse; to *diffuse* is to spread something out: "Bob's cheap cologne diffused throughout the room, wrecking the wine tasting."

Commonly Confused Words

Degrade / Denigrate / Downgrade
To *degrade* can be to lower in status or rank, or to corrupt or make contemptible; but it always has to do with reduction in value. To *denigrate* is to defame. When something is *downgraded*, it is lowered in value.

Depreciate / Deprecate
To *depreciate* something is to actually make it worse, whereas to *deprecate* something is simply to speak or think of it in a manner that demonstrates your low opinion of it.

> **"Anyone who goes to a psychiatrist ought to have his head examined."**
>
> Samuel Goldwyn

Desert / Dessert
A *desert* is a dry area with lots of sand. A *dessert* is what we eat after a meal that tastes great. Where it gets tricky is when you say that someone is getting their just deserts. It is spelled like the place and pronounced like the food, and means deserved punishment or reward.

Device / Devise
Device is a noun. A can opener is a device. *Devise* is a verb. You can devise a plan for opening a can with a sharp rock instead. Only in law is "devise" properly used as a noun, meaning something deeded in a will.

Differ / Vary
To *differ* is "to be unlike or distinct in nature." To *vary* is "to make different." *Vary* can mean *differ*, but saying "Our opinions vary" makes it sound as if they were changing all the time when what you really mean is "Our opinions differ." Pay attention to context when choosing one of these words.

Dilemma / Difficulty
A *dilemma* is a difficult choice, not just any difficulty or problem. Whether to invite your son's mother to his high school graduation when your current wife hates her is a dilemma. Cleaning up after a hurricane is a *difficulty*.

Disburse / Disperse
You *disburse* money by taking it out of your purse (French "bourse") and distributing it. If you refuse to hand out any money, the eager mob of beggars before you may *disperse* (scatter).

Disc / Disk
Compact disc is spelled with a "c" because that's how its inventors decided it should be spelled; but a computer *disk* is spelled with a "k" (unless it's a CD-ROM, of course). The *New York Times* insisted for many years on the spelling *compact disk* in its editorial pages, often incongruously next to ads containing the copyrighted spelling *disc*; but now even it has given in.

Discomfort / Discomfit
Discomfort means "uneasiness or hardship" and to "make uncomfortable." *Discomfit* means "disconcert" and "defeat; thwart."

Discrete / Discreet
Discrete is an adjective that means separate or individually distinct. "Each child in the family has a discrete personality." *Discreet* is an adjective that means prudent, circumspect, or modest: "Her discreet handling of the touchy situation was very much appreciated."

Discussed / Disgust
Discussed is the past tense of the verb "discuss." Don't substitute for it the noun *disgust* (an aversion to) in such sentences as "The couple's wedding plans were thoroughly discussed."

Commonly Confused Words

Disinterested / Uninterested

Disinterested is an adjective that means unbiased or impartial. This use is rarer, but is often confused with *uninterested*, which simply means not interested, or bored.

Dribble / Drivel

Dribble means an insignificant amount. *Drivel* has two legitimate meanings: one is to let saliva dribble from the mouth, and the other is to talk stupidly.

Drier / Dryer

Drier is an adjective meaning less wet; *dryer* is a noun that names a machine to dry clothes. A clothes *dryer* makes the clothes *drier*.

Dual / Duel

Dual is an adjective describing the two-ness of something—dual carburetors, for instance. A *duel* is a formal battle intended to settle a dispute.

Dyeing / Dying

If you are using dye to change your favorite t-shirt from white to blue you are *dyeing* it; but if you don't breathe for so long that your face turns blue, you may be *dying*.

Ecology / Environment

Ecology is the study of living things in relationship to their environment. The word can also be used to describe the totality of such relationships; but it should not be substituted for *environment* in statements like "improperly discarded lead batteries harm the ecology."

Economical / Economic

Something is *economical* if it saves you money; but if you're talking about the effect of some measure on the world's economy, it's an *economic* effect.

e.g. / i.e.

When you mean "for example," use *e.g.* It is an abbreviation for the Latin phrase exempli gratia. When you mean "that is," use *i.e.* It is an abbreviation for the Latin phrase id est. Either can be used to clarify a preceding statement, the first by example, the second by restating the idea more clearly or expanding upon it. Because these uses are so similar, the two abbreviations are easily confused. You may want to simply use "for example" and "that is." If you insist on using the abbreviation, perhaps "example given" will remind you to use *e.g.*, while "in effect" suggests *i.e.*

> **"It is unfortunate that it [Watergate] happened, but people are using it as a political football to bury my brother."**
>
> Donald Nixon, brother to President Richard Nixon

Elapse / Lapse

Both these words come from a Latin root meaning "to slip." *Elapse* almost always refers to the passage of time. *Lapse* usually refers to a change of state, as in lapsing from consciousness into unconsciousness.

Commonly Confused Words

Electrocute / Shock

To *electrocute* is to kill using electricity. If you live to tell the tale, you've been *shocked*, but not electrocuted. The phrase "electrocuted to death" is a redundancy.

Elicit / Illicit

Elicit is a verb that means to draw out. *Illicit* is an adjective meaning unlawful. "No matter how I tried to elicit the juicy details, he kept silent on the details of illicit activities."

Emigrate / Immigrate

To *emigrate* is to leave a country. The "e" at the beginning of the word is related to the "e" in other words having to do with going out, such as "exit." *Immigrate*, in contrast, looks as if it might have something to do with going in, and indeed it does: it means to move into a new country. The same distinction applies to *emigration* and *immigration*. Note the double "m" in the second form. A migrant is someone who continually moves about.

Eminent / Imminent / Immanent

By far the most common of these words is *eminent*, meaning "prominent, famous." *Imminent*, in phrases like "facing imminent disaster," means "threatening." It comes from Latin minere, meaning "to project or overhang." The rarest of the three is *immanent*, used by philosophers to mean "inherent" and by theologians to mean "present throughout the universe."

> **"I stand by all the misstatements that I've made."**
>
> President George W. Bush

Empathy / Sympathy

If you think you feel just like another person, you are feeling *empathy*. If you just feel sorry for another person, you're feeling *sympathy*.

Commonly Confused Words

Energize / Enervate

Energize means "give energy to," while *enervate* means "to cause to lose vitality or energy." Sometimes these are used interchangeably, but they are actually opposites.

Enquire / Inquire

These are alternative spellings of the same word. *Enquire* is perhaps slightly more common in the U.K., but either is acceptable in the U.S.

Envelop / Envelope

To wrap something up in a covering is to *envelop* it (pronounced "en-VELL-up"). The specific wrapping you put around a letter is an *envelope* (pronounced variously, but with the accent on the first syllable).

Envious / Jealous

Although these are often treated as synonyms, there is a difference. You are *envious* of what others have that you lack. *Jealousy,* on the other hand, involves wanting to hold on to what you do have. You can be jealous of your boyfriend's attraction to other women, but you're envious of your boyfriend's CD collection.

Epitaph / Epithet

An *epitaph* is the inscription on a tombstone or some other tribute to a dead person. An *epithet* is a term used to characterize the nature of a person or thing, perhaps even coming to form part of the person's name or title. An example would be "Richard the Lion-Hearted."

Exalt / Exult

When you raise something high (even if only in your opinion), you *exalt* it. When you celebrate joyfully, you *exult*. Neither word has an "h" in it.

Exceptional / Exceptionable

If you take exception (object) to something, you find it *exceptionable*. The more common word is *exceptional*, applied to things that are out of the ordinary, usually in a positive way: "These are exceptional Buffalo wings."

Expand / Expound

Expand means simply to enlarge; *expound* means to explain in detail.

Explicit / Implicit

Explicit means deliberately spelled out. *Implicit* means to be not directly stated, but strongly suggested or implied.

Famous / Infamous

To be *famous* is to be well known, usually for positive reasons. To be *infamous* is to be widely known in a negative way.

Farther / Further

Farther is an adjective and adverb that means a physical distance. "We drove 50 miles today; tomorrow, we will travel 100 miles farther." *Further* is an adjective and adverb that means a figurative distance. "We won't be able to suggest a solution until we are further along in our evaluation of the problem." It can also mean in addition or moreover: "They stated further that they would not change the policy."

Faze / Phase

Faze means to embarrass or disturb, as in "The loud noise didn't faze her." *Phase* is a noun when it means one portion of a process: "He's going through a difficult phase." It is a verb when it means to carry out in planned stages: "They're going to phase in the new accounting procedures gradually."

Few / Less

Few is an adjective that is used with countable objects: "There are only a few people here today." *Less* is an adjective used with more generalized amounts. "Which jar holds less water?"

Figuratively / Literally

Figuratively is an adverb that means metaphorically or symbolically: "Figuratively speaking, we died laughing." *Literally* is an adverb that means actually: "I'm not exaggerating when I say I literally fell off my chair." It also means according to the exact meaning of the words: "I translated the Latin passage literally."

Fiscal / Physical

Fiscal refers to "taxation, public revenues, or public debt." *Physical* means "perceptible through the senses." The middle syllable of the latter is often omitted in pronunciation, making the two words incorrectly sound related.

> **"Cocaine isn't habit forming. I should know – I've been using it for years."**
>
> Talullah Bankhead

Flair / Flare

Flair is conspicuous talent: "She has a flair for organization." *Flare* is a noun meaning "a blaze of light."

Flaunt / Flout

To *flaunt* means to show off shamelessly: "Eager to flaunt her knowledge of a wide range of topics, Helene dreamed of appearing on a TV trivia show." To *flout* means to show scorn or contempt for: "Lewis disliked boarding school and took every opportunity to flout the house rules."

Footnotes / Endnotes

Footnotes are printed at the bottom of each page. *Endnotes* are found at the ends of chapters, books, or papers.

For / Fore / Four

The most common member of this trio is the preposition *for*, which is not a problem for most people. *Fore* always has to do with the front of something. It's also what you shout to warn someone when you've sent a golf ball their way. *Four* is just the number "4."

> **"It isn't pollution that's harming the environment. It's the impurities in our air and water that are doing it."**
>
> Former Vice President Dan Quayle

Forbidding / Foreboding

Forbidding is "hostile or dangerous." "He cast a forbidding glance at us." *Foreboding* means "ominous," as in "The sky was a foreboding shade of gray."

Forego / Forgo

The "e" in *forego* tells you it has to do with going before. It occurs mainly in the expression "foregone conclusion," an opinion arrived at in advance. *Forgo* means "to abstain from or do without."

Foreword / Forward

Foreword is a noun that means an introductory note or preface: "In my foreword I explained my reasons for writing the book." *Forward* is an adjective or adverb that means toward the front: "Please step forward when your name is called." *Forward* is also a verb that means to send on: "Forward the letter to the customer's new address."

Formally / Formerly

If you are doing something in a proper manner, you are behaving *formally*. If you did something previously, you did so *formerly*.

Forte / Forte

Forte, pronounced FORT, means someone's specialty or what they are best at. *Forte*, pronounced for-TAY, is a musical term meaning "loudly." Many people use the for-TAY pronunciation for both uses.

Fortuitous / Fortunate

Fortuitous events happen by chance; they need not be *fortunate* (lucky) events, only random ones: "It was purely fortuitous that the meter reader came along five minutes before I returned to my car."

Foul / Fowl

A *fowl* is a bird. When something is *foul,* it is offensive or against the rules.

Founder / Flounder

Founder means "to fail completely." Often it is used to refer to a ship, in which case it means, "to fill with water and sink." *Flounder* has a less severe definition; it means "to move clumsily or with difficulty."

Gaff / Gaffe

Gaffe is a French word meaning "embarrassing mistake," and should not be mixed up with *gaff*, a large hook.

Gamut / Gauntlet

To *run a gamut* is to go through the whole scale or spectrum of something. To *run the gauntlet* (also gantlet) is to run between two lines of people who are trying to beat you.

Gibe / Jibe / Jive

Gibe is a now rare term meaning "to tease." *Jibe* means "to agree," but is usually used negatively, as in "The alibis of the two crooks didn't jibe." *Jive* has come to be mean "to deceive," as in "Don't give me any jive."

Gild / Guild

You *gild* an object by covering it with gold; a *guild* is a group of people with similar interests, like the Theatre Guild.

Good / Well

Good is the adjective; *well* is the adverb. You do something well, but something is good. "The good boy played his trumpet well."

Gratis / Gratuitous

If you do something nice without being paid, you do it *gratis*. Technically, such a deed can also be *gratuitous*, unearned or unjustified.

Grisly / Grizzly

Grisly means "horrible"; a *grizzly* is a bear. "The grizzly left behind the grisly remains of his victim."

Hanged / Hung

Hang means to execute by suspending by the neck: "They hanged the prisoner for treason." *Hung* is to suspend from above with no support from below: "I hung the painting on the wall." People hang, things get hung.

Hardy / Hearty

Hardy is bold or brazen. *Heart* means "enthusiastic endorsement." These two words overlap somewhat, but usually the word you want is *hearty*.

Commonly Confused Words

Hear / Here

Hear means "to perceive by the ear." It even has the word "ear" buried in it. *Here* indicates location: "I left my wallet here" is the correct expression.

Hero / Protagonist

In ordinary usage, *hero* has two meanings: "leading character in a story," and "brave, admirable person." A *protagonist* is also a "leading character," but he may behave in a very unheroic way. See also "heroin/heroine."

Heroin / Heroine

Heroin is a highly addictive opium derivative; the main female character in a narrative is a *heroine*.

> **"Outside of the killings, Washington has one of the lowest crime rates in the country."**
>
> Mayor Marion Barry

Hippie / Hippy

A long-haired 60s flower child is a *hippie*. *Hippy* is an adjective describing someone with wide hips.

Historic / Historical

In general usage, *historic* refers to what is important in history, while *historical* applies more broadly to whatever existed in the past whether it was important or not: "a historic summit meeting between the prime ministers"; "historical buildings torn down in the redevelopment."

Hoard / Horde

A greedily hoarded treasure is a *hoard*. A herd of wild beasts or a mob of people is a *horde*.

Hysterical / Hilarious

People say of a bit of humor or a comical situation that it was *hysterical,* meaning *hilarious.* But when you speak of a man being *hysterical* it means he is having a fit of hysteria, and that may not be funny at all.

Idea / Ideal

Any thought can be an *idea,* but only the best ideas worth pursuing are *ideals.*

Ignorant / Stupid

A person can be *ignorant* (not knowing some fact or idea) without being *stupid* (incapable of learning).

> **"The first ninety minutes of a football match are the most important."**
>
> Bobby Robson,
> Football manager

Imply / Infer

Imply means to "hint or suggest without stating directly." *Infer* means "reach an opinion from facts or reasoning." The sender of an indirectly stated message is doing the implying, while a receiver that reasons what the message is, is doing the inferring.

In / Into

In means a state of being within (at rest). *Into* means movement to a place (in motion).

Inanity / Inanition

Inanity means "foolishness" or "senselessness." *Inanition* means "lacking vigor."

Incent / Incentivize

Business folks sometimes use *incent* to mean "create an incentive," but it is not standard English. *Incentivize* is even more widely used, but strikes many people as an ugly substitute for "encourage."

Incidence / Incidents / Instances

These three overlap in meaning just enough to confuse a lot of people. Few of us have a need for *incidence,* which most often indicates the occurrence of something ("The incidence of measles in Whitman County has dropped markedly since the vaccine has been provided free"). Its plural form is *incidents. Instances* are examples, as in, "for instance."

Incredulous / Incredible

Incredulous means "skeptical." *Incredible* means "unbelievable" or "hard to believe." If something incredible happens, you may be incredulous.

Ingenious / Ingenuous

Ingenious means "clever and inventive." *Ingenuous* means "open, frank, and sincere" and also "naive, unsophisticated." The words have similar origins, hence the similar spelling, but their meanings have been distinct for centuries.

Install / Instill

To *install* is to "establish in an indicated place." To *instill* is to "impart gradually." You *install* equipment, you *instill* feelings or attitudes.

Intense / Intensive

If you are putting forth a concentrated effort, your work is *intense*: "My intense study of Plato convinced me that I would make a good leader." But when the intensity stems more from external rather than internal forces, the usual word is *intensive*: "The village endured intensive bombing."

Interment / Internment

Interment is burial; *internment* is merely imprisonment.

Commonly Confused Words

Internet / Intranet

Internet is the proper name of the network most people connect to, and the word needs to be capitalized. However *intranet*, a network confined to a smaller group, is a generic term which does not deserve capitalization.

Ironically / Coincidentally

An event that is strikingly different from what one would have expected is *ironic*: "The sheriff proclaimed a zero-tolerance policy on drugs, but ironically flunked his own test." Other striking comings-together of events are merely *coincidental*: "The lovers leapt off the tower just as a hay wagon coincidentally passed below."

Itch / Scratch

Strictly speaking, you *scratch* an *itch*. If you're trying to get rid of a tingly feeling on your back scratch it, don't itch it.

It's / Its

It's is a contraction for *it is*, whereas *its* is the possessive form of it: "It's a shame that we cannot talk about its size."

Jerry-built / Jury-rigged

These are two distinct expressions. Something poorly built is *jerry-built*. Something rigged up temporarily in a makeshift manner with materials at hand, often in an ingenious manner, is *jury-rigged*. *Jerry-built* always has a negative connotation, whereas one can be impressed by the cleverness of a jury-rigged solution.

Laid / Lain / Lay

Laid is the past tense and the past participle of the verb lay and not the past tense of lie. *Lay* is the past tense of the verb lie and lain is the past participle: "He laid his books down and lay down on the couch, where he has lain for an hour."

Lay / Lie

Lay means "to place something"; it indicates motion. *Lie* means "to be at rest," and suggests a state of being. You lay down the book you've been reading, but you lie down when you go to bed.

Leach / Leech

To *leach* is "to dissolve out by a percolating liquid." To *leech* is "to drain the substance of." Water *leaches* chemicals out of soil or color out of cloth; your brother-in-law *leeches* off the family by constantly borrowing money.

> **"Sure there have been injuries and deaths in boxing—but none of them serious."**
>
> Alan Minter

Leave / Let

The colloquial use of *leave* to mean *let* in phrases like "leave me be" is not standard. "Leave me alone" is fine, though.

Lend / Loan

Although some people feel *loan* should only be used as a noun, *lend* and *loan* are both acceptable as verbs in standard English: "Can you lend (loan) me a dollar?" However, only lend should be used in figurative senses: "Will you lend me a hand?"

Liable / Libel

Liable means legally obligated or responsible. *Libel* is printed or written material that damages a person by defaming his character or exposes him to ridicule.

Lightening / Lightning

Lightening is a verb that means to illuminate; *lightning* is a noun referring to the electrical charges that cause flashes of light during storms: "The lightning struck, lightening the sky."

Loath / Loathe

Loath is an adjective, meaning "disinclined" or "reluctant." *Loathe* is a verb, meaning "to feel hatred or disgust for." Confusion often arises about not only what they mean but how they are pronounced. *Loath* has a soft "th" sound, while *loathe* has a hard "th" sound.

Lusty / Lustful

Lusty means "brimming with vigor and good health" or "enthusiastic." Don't confuse it with *lustful*, which means "filled with sexual desire."

Luxurious / Luxuriant

Luxurious means "supplied with luxuries." *Luxuriant* means "growing profusely."

Mantle / Mantel

Though they stem from the same word, a *mantle* today is usually a cloak, while the shelf over a fireplace is most often spelled *mantel*.

> **"All generalizations are bad."**
>
> R.H. Grenier

Marital / Martial

Marital refers to marriage, *martial* to war. These two words are often swapped, with comical results.

Masseuse / Masseur

Masseuse is a strictly female term; Monsieur Philippe, who gives back rubs down at the men's gym, is a *masseur*. Because of the unsavory associations that have gathered around the term *masseuse*, serious practitioners generally prefer to be called "massage therapists."

May / Might

Most of the time *may* and *might* are almost interchangeable, with *might* suggesting a somewhat lower probability. But *might* is also the past tense of the auxiliary verb *may*, and is required in sentences like "Chuck might have avoided arrest for the robbery if he hadn't given the teller his business card before asking for the money." When speculating that events might have been other than they were, don't substitute *may* for *might*.

Medal / Metal / Meddle/ Mettle

When we win a contest, we earn a *medal*. *Metal* is any of a category of electropositive elements that usually have a shiny surface, are generally conductors of heat and electricity, and can be melted or fused, hammered into sheets, etc. *Meddle* is a verb meaning to intrude into other people's affairs. A person who proves his or her *mettle* displays courage or stamina. The word *mettle* is seldom used outside of this expression, so people constantly confuse it with other similar-sounding words.

Metaphor / Simile

Both of these words refer to figures of speech that compare seemingly unlike things to each other. *Metaphors* do this indirectly, by implying a comparison, such as in Shakespeare's famous "All the world's a stage." *Similes* make the comparison directly with the use of words such as "like" or "as." An example would be another of Shakespeare's quotes, "So are you to my thoughts as food to life."

Moral / Morale

If you are trying to make people behave properly, you are policing their *morals*; if you are just trying to keep their spirits up, you are trying to maintain their *morale*. *Moral* is accented on the first syllable, *morale* on the second.

Motion / Move

When you make a *motion* in a meeting, say simply "I *move*," as in "I move to adjourn"; if you're taking the minutes, write "Barbara moved," not "Barbara motioned" (unless Barbara was making wild arm-waving gestures to summon the servers to bring in the lunch). Instead of "I want to make a motion . . ." it's simpler and more direct to say "I want to move. . . ."

Mucous / Mucus

Mucous is an adjective, usually used to describe a gland: "mucous glands." *Mucus* is a noun used to describe the substance that comes from a gland: "There is mucus coming from the baby's nose."

Myriad of / Myriad

Some traditionalists object to the word "of" after *myriad* or an "a" before, though both are fairly common in formal writing. The word means "a great many."

Nauseous / Nauseated

Nauseous means causing nausea or disgust (as does "nauseating") and *nauseated* means feeling nausea or disgust. There is some disagreement about whether it is correct to use *nauseous* to mean feeling *nauseated*. While *Webster's* says it is correct, it is more common to stick to *nauseous* for causing, and *nauseated* for feeling nausea.

Nerve-wracking / Nerve-racking / Nerve-wrecking

The first two entries are both acceptable, and mean distressing or irritating to the nerves. There is no such word as nerve-wrecking.

Noisome / Noisy

Noisome means "harmful" or "offensive" or "disgusting." It does not share any part of its meaning with *noisy*, meaning to "make clamor."

Onto / On to

If you mean on top of something or aware of it, use *onto*: "I'm onto your tricks." *On* should be used in all other cases: "The discussion moved on to other things."

Oppress / Repress

Oppression is always bad, and implies serious persecution. "The citizens were oppressed by the new taxes." *Repress* just means "keep under control." Sometimes repression is a good thing: "During the job interview, repress the temptation to tell Mr. Brown that he has toilet paper stuck to his shoe."

"For your information, I would like to ask a question."

Samuel Goldwyn

Ordinance / Ordnance

A law is an *ordinance,* but a gun is a piece of *ordnance.*

Oriental / Asian

Oriental is generally considered old-fashioned now, and many find it offensive. *Asian* is the preferred term, but it is better still to use the nationality involved, for example, "Chinese" or "Indian," if you know it.

Overdo / Overdue

If you *overdo* (use in excess) the cocktails after work you may be *overdue* (delayed) for your daughter's soccer game at 6:00.

Commonly Confused Words

Oversee / Overlook
When you *oversee* the preparation of dinner, you take control and manage the operation closely. But if you *overlook* the preparation of dinner you fail to prepare the meal entirely.

> **"Only one man ever understood me, and he didn't understand me."**
> G.W. Hegel

Palate / Palette / Pallet
Your *palate* is the roof of your mouth, and by extension, your sense of taste. A *palette* is the flat board an artist mixes paint on (or by extension, a range of colors). A *pallet* is a flat platform onto which goods are loaded.

Paralyzation / Paralysis
Some people derive the noun *paralyzation* from the verb *paralyze*, but the proper term is *paralysis*.

Passed / Past
Passed is a past tense verb. *Past* can be a noun, adjective, adverb, or preposition, but never a verb. *Passed* is the past tense and past participle of pass. *Past* refers to time gone by. "In the past decade, I passed over countless opportunities; I was determined not to let them get past me again."

Peace / Piece
Peace means "a state of tranquility." A *piece* is "a fragment" of a whole object.

Peak / Peek / Pique
A *peak* is the highest point, as in the peak of a mountain. To *peek* means "to take a brief look." *Pique* is a French word meaning "prick," in the sense of "stimulate." Therefore we hear the expression, "My curiosity was piqued."

Commonly Confused Words

Peasant / Pheasant

In the former Soviet Union, farm workers are still called *peasants.* That word is no relation to *pheasant,* a favorite game bird.

Peccable / Peccant

Peccable means capable of committing a sin or moral offense. *Peccant* means guilty of a sin or moral offense.

Penultimate / Last

Meaning "next to last," *penultimate* is often mistakenly used to mean "the very last," or the ultimate: "The perfectionist was crestfallen when he was awarded the penultimate prize; the grand prize went to another." Many people also mistakenly use *penultimate* when they mean "quintessential" or "archetypical."

Perpetuate / Perpetrate

Perpetrate is something criminals do (criminals are sometimes called "perps" in cop slang). When you seek to continue something you are trying to *perpetuate* it.

Persecute / Prosecute

When you *persecute* someone, you're treating them badly, whether they deserve it or not; only legal officers can *prosecute* someone for a crime.

Personal / Personnel

Individuals have characteristics that are particular to them. These are *personal* traits. Employees are *personnel.*

> **"I didn't really say everything I said."**
>
> Yogi Berra

Perspective / Prospective

Perspective has to do with objects in proportionate size to each other, as in a painting. *Prospective* generally has to do with the future ("What are your prospects, young man?"). There is also a fairly common meaning of the word "prospect" that has to do with sight: "The prospect of his death alarmed him."

Perspicacious / Perspicuous

Perspicacious means "having or showing insight." *Perspicuous* means "easily understood" or "lucid," or, when referring to a person, "expressing things clearly."

Philippines / Filipinos

The people of the *Philippines* are called *Filipinos*. Don't switch the initial letters of these two words.

Picaresque / Picturesque

Picaresque is a technical literary term that labels a sort of literature involving a picaro (Spanish), a lovable rogue who roams the land having colorful adventures. A landscape that looks as lovely as a picture is *picturesque*.

Picture / Pitcher

A *picture* is a likeness of something or someone, either drawn, painted, or photographed. A *pitcher* is a container for liquids.

Plug / Outlet

Some people incorrectly refer to the receptacle in the wall as a plug. That thing on the end of an electrical cord is a *plug*, which goes into the socket of the wall *outlet*.

Podium / Lectern

Strictly speaking, a *podium* is a raised platform on which you stand to give a speech; the piece of furniture on which you place your notes and behind which you stand is a *lectern*.

Pole / Poll

A *pole* is a long stick. You could take a *poll* (survey or ballot) to determine whether voters want lower taxes or better education.

Pompom / Pompon

To most people that fuzzy ball on the top of a knit hat and the implement wielded by a cheerleader are both *pompoms*, but to traditionalists they are *pompons*, spelled the way the French do.

> **"Of course I can keep secrets. It's the people I tell them to that can't keep them."**
>
> Anthony Hadenb-Guest

Populace / Populous

The population of a country may be referred to as its *populace*, but a crowded country is *populous*.

Pore / Pour

When used as a verb, *pore* has the unusual sense of "scrutinize," as in "She pored over her receipts." But a liquid *pours* out of its container.

Practicable / Practical

Practicable means "usable," while *practical* means "useful." Not all practicable things are practical, and not all practical things are practicable.

Practice / Practise

In the United Kingdom, *practice* is the noun, *practise* the verb; but in the U.S. the spelling *practice* is commonly used for both, though the distinction is sometimes observed. *Practise* as a noun is, however, always wrong in both places: a doctor always has a *practice*, never a *practise*.

Pray / Prey

If you want a miracle, *pray* to God. If you're a criminal, you *prey* on your victims. Incidentally, it's "praying mantis," not "preying mantis." The insect holds its forefeet in a position suggesting prayer.

> **"I believe we are on an irreversible trend toward more freedom and democracy—but that could change."**
>
> Former Vice President Dan Quayle

Precede / Proceed

Precede means "to go before." *Proceed* means to go on. "Let your companion precede you through the door, then proceed to follow her."

Precedence / Precedents

Although these words sound the same, they work differently. The pop star is given *precedence* (special treatment) over the factory worker at the dance club. *Precedents* is just the plural of *precedent* (an action that sets an example to follow later): "If we let the kids adopt that rattlesnake as a pet, we'll be setting some bad precedents."

Precipitate / Precipitous

If you make a *precipitate* decision, you are making a hasty and probably unwise one. If the stock market declines *precipitously* it goes down sharply. Both of these adjectives are based on the image of plunging over the brink of a precipice, but *precipitate* emphasizes the suddenness of the plunge, *precipitous*, the steepness of it.

Predominate / Predominant

Predominate is a verb meaning "to have greater power or importance than others": "In the royal throne room, the color red predominates." *Predominant* is an adjective, meaning "most conspicuous": "The predominant view is that Fancy Dancer is the best bet in the third race."

Premier / Premiere

These words are, respectively, the masculine and feminine forms of the word for "first" in French, but they have become differentiated in English. Only the masculine form is used as an adjective, as in "Tidy-Pool is the premier pool-cleaning firm in Orange County." The confusion arises when these words are used as nouns. The prime minister of a parliamentary government is known as a *premier.* The opening night of a film or play is its *premiere. Premiere* as a verb is common in the arts and in show business ("The show premiered on PBS"), but it is less acceptable in other contexts.

Premise / Premises

Some people suppose that since *premises* has a plural form, a single house or other piece of property must be a *premise.* But that word is reserved for use as a term in logic meaning something assumed or taken as given in making an argument. Your property is still your *premises.*

Prescribe / Proscribe

You recommend something when you *prescribe* it, but you forbid it when you *proscribe* it.

Presently / Currently

Some argue that *presently* doesn't mean "in the present." It means "soon." If you want to talk about something that's happening right now, say it's going on *currently.*

Pretty / Somewhat

It's pretty common to use *pretty* to mean "somewhat" in ordinary speech, but it should be avoided in formal writing, where sometimes "very" is more appropriate.

Commonly Confused Words

Principal / Principle

Principal is a noun that means a person who holds a high position or plays an important role: "The school principal has 20 years of teaching experience." *Principal* is also an adjective that means chief or leading: "The necessity of moving to another city was the principal reason I turned down the job offer." *Principle* is a noun that means a rule or standard: "They refused to compromise their principles."

Prone / Supine

Prone (face down) is often confused with *supine* (face up). Prostrate technically also means "face down," but is most often used to mean simply "devastated."

> **"I don't care how much a man talks, if he only says it in a few words."**
>
> Josh Billings

Prophecy / Prophesy

Prophecy, the noun, is a prediction. The verb *to prophesy* means to predict something. When a prophet prophesies he or she utters prophecies.

Prostate / Prostrate

The gland men have is called the *prostate. Prostrate* is an adjective meaning "lying face downward."

Proved / Proven

For most purposes either form is a fine past participle of "prove," though in a phrase like "a proven talent" where the word is an adjective preceding a noun, *proven* is standard.

Purposely / Purposefully

If you do something on purpose (not by accident), you do it *purposely.* But if you have a specific purpose in mind, you are acting *purposefully.*

Commonly Confused Words

Quiet / Quite

One often sees *quiet* (shhh!) substituted for *quite* (very). This is one of those common errors your spelling checker will not catch, so look out for it.

Rack / Wrack

If you are racked with pain or you feel nerve-racked, you are feeling as if you were being stretched on that Medieval instrument of torture, the *rack*. *Wrack* has to do with ruinous accidents, so if the stock market is wracked by rumors of imminent recession, it's wrecked.

Rationale / Rationalization

When you're explaining the reasoning behind your position, you're presenting your *rationale*. But if you're just making up some lame excuse to make your position appear better, you're engaging in *rationalization*.

Reactionary / Reactive

Reactive means "acting in response to some outside stimulus." *Reactionary* actually has a very narrow meaning: it is a noun or adjective describing a form of looking backward, wanting to recreate a lost past. The advocates of restoring Czarist rule in Russia are reactionaries.

Real / Really

The correct adverbial form is *really* rather than *real*; but even that form is generally confined to casual speech, as in "When you complimented me on my speech I felt really great!" However "really" is a feeble qualifier. "Wonderful" is an acceptable substitute for "really great." Usually it is better to replace the expression altogether with something more precise.

Commonly Confused Words

Rebel / Revolt

Even though *rebel* and *revolt* mean more or less the same thing, people who are revolting are disgusting, not taking up arms against the government.

Rebut / Refute

When you *rebut* someone's argument you argue against it. To *refute* someone's argument is to prove it incorrect. Unless you are certain you have achieved success, use *rebut.*

> **"I haven't committed a crime. What I did was fail to comply with the law."**
>
> David Dinkins,
> Former New York city Mayor

Recent / Resent

Recent means "not long ago": "I appreciated your recent encouragement." *Resent* has two meanings, the first being "to feel bad about": "I resent Tom's implication about the money." The second means "to send again": "The e-mail came back, so I resent it."

Recuperate / Recoup

If you are getting over an illness, you are *recuperating;* but if you insist on remaining at the roulette table when your luck has been running against you, you are seeking to *recoup* your losses.

Remuneration / Renumeration

Although *remuneration* looks as if it might mean "repayment," it usually means simply "payment." In speech it is often confused with *renumeration,* re-counting (counting again).

Repel / Repulse

In most of their meanings these are synonyms, but if you are disgusted by someone, you are *repelled,* not repulsed. The confusion is compounded by the fact that "repellent" and "repulsive" mean the same thing.

Resister / Resistor

A person who resists something is a *resister*. A *resistor* is part of an electrical circuit.

Retch / Wretch

If you vomit, you *retch*; if you behave badly and fall into miserable circumstances, you are a *wretch*.

Revue / Review

You can attend a musical *revue* in a theatre, but when you write up your reactions for a newspaper, you're writing a *review*.

Risky / Risqué

People unfamiliar with the French-derived word *risqué* (slightly indecent) often write *risky* by mistake. Bungee-jumping is *risky*, but nude bungee-jumping is *risqué*.

Role / Roll

An actor plays a *role*. Bill Gates is the entrepreneur's role model. But you eat a sausage on a *roll* and *roll* out the barrel.

Root / Rout / Route

You can *root* for your team (cheer them on), and hope that they utterly smash their opponents (create a *rout*), then come back in triumph on *Route* 27 (a road).

Sail / Sale / Sell

These simple and familiar words are surprisingly often confused in writing. You *sail* a boat which has a sail of canvas. You *sell* your old fondue pot at a yard *sale*.

Sanguine / Sanguinary

Sanguine means "hopeful," "optimistic," or "confident." *Sanguinary* means "bloody" or "murderous."

Commonly Confused Words

Sarcastic / Ironic

Sarcasm is language meant to mock or wound. *Irony* can be amusing without being maliciously aimed at hurting anyone.

Seam / Seem

Seam is a noun when it means the line produced when two pieces of cloth are sewn together. *Seem* is a verb meaning "to give the impression of being.

Self-worth / Self-esteem

To say that a person has a low sense of *self-worth* makes sense, but people usually shorten the phrase to, "He has low self-worth." This would literally mean that he isn't worth much rather than that he has a low opinion of himself. *Self-esteem* is a more precise term.

Sense / Since

Sense is a verb meaning "feel" ("I sense you near me") or a noun meaning "intelligence" ("have some common sense!"). Don't use it when you need the adverb *since* ("I haven't seen him since Tuesday.").

> **"The best cure for insomnia is to get a lot of sleep."**
>
> W.C. Fields

Set / Sit

In some dialects people say "Come on in and set a spell," but in standard English the word is *sit*. You *set* down an object or a child you happen to be carrying; but those seating themselves *sit*.

Shall / Will

Will has almost entirely replaced *shall* in American English except in legal documents and in questions like "Shall we have red wine with the duck?"

Silicon / Silicone

Silicon is a chemical element, the basic stuff of which microchips are made. Sand is largely silicon. *Silicones* are plastics and other materials containing silicon.

Sojourn / Journey

Although the spelling of this word confuses many people into thinking it means "journey," a *sojourn* is actually a temporary stay in one place. If you're constantly on the move, you're not engaged in a sojourn.

> **"If you live to the age of a hundred, you have it made because very few people die past the age of a hundred."**
>
> George Burns

Stanch / Staunch

Stanch is a verb that means to stop a flow. *Staunch* is an adjective that means firm in opinion or loyalty. Both words are pronounced the same way (STONCH).

Stationary / Stationery

Stationary is an adjective that means to stay in one place or not moving. *Stationery* is a noun that means writing materials, usually referring to writing paper and matching envelopes. "I rode my stationary bike while writing a letter to my mom on my stationery."

Stomp / Stamp

Stomp is colloquial, casual. A professional wrestler stomps his opponent. In more formal contexts *stamp* is preferred.

Commonly Confused Words

Suit / Suite

A *suit* is a set of garments or a costume. A suite is a collection or group of things forming a unit. Your bedroom *suite* consists of the bed, the nightstand, and whatever other furniture goes with it. Your pajamas would be your bedroom *suit*.

Summery / Summary

When the weather is warm and *summery* (summer-like), you don't feel like spending a lot of time reading that long report from the restructuring committee. Just read the *summary* (the short version).

Taunt / Taut / Tout

Taunt ("tease" or "mock") can be a verb or noun, but never an adjective. *Taut* means "tight, distended," and is always an adjective. *Tout* means "to promote," as in "Senator Butterworth has been touted as a Presidential candidate." You *tout* somebody you admire and *taunt* someone that you don't.

Tenant / Tenet

These two words come from the same Latin root, "tenere," meaning "to hold"; but they have very different meanings. *Tenet* is the rarer of the two, meaning a belief that a person holds: "Avoiding pork is a tenet of the Muslim faith." In contrast, the person leasing an apartment from you is your *tenant*. (She holds the lease.)

Than / Then

When comparing one thing with another you may find that one is more appealing than another. *Than* is the word you want when doing comparisons. But if you are talking about time, choose *then*: "First you separate the eggs; *then* you beat the whites." Alexis is smarter *than* I, not "then I."

That / Which

Most people do not strictly observe this distinction. However, there is a fine difference between these two words. *That* is widely used for clauses that are essential to the meaning of the sentence. "A candidate that is not supported by his party will not succeed." *That* is used to introduce information to tell specifically which candidate is being mentioned. *Which* is used to introduce information that is not absolutely essential to the meaning of the sentence. "The candidate, which received his party's endorsement, is rated high in the polls." The information within the commas is not essential to the primary part of the sentence: "The candidate is rated high in the polls." So in this case, *which* is the appropriate choice.

Their / There / They're

Their is the possessive form of they; *there* refers to place; and *they're* is the contraction of they are. "They're going there because their mother insisted they become proficient in Serbo-Croatian."

Them / Those

One use of *them* for *those* has become a standard catch phrase: "How do you like them apples?" This is deliberate dialectical humor. But "I like them little canapés with the shrimp on top" is incorrect; say instead "I like those little canapés."

They're / Their / There

There is always a contraction of *they are. Their* is a possessive pronoun like "her" or "our": "They eat their hotdogs with sauerkraut." Everything else is *there*. "There goes the ball, out of the park!"

Throne / Thrown

A *throne* is that chair a king sits on, at least until he gets *thrown* out of office.

Titillate / Titivate

Titillate means "stimulate pleasantly" or "tickle." *Titivate* means "adorn" or "spruce up."

To / Too / Two

People seldom mix *two* up with the other two; it obviously belongs with words that also begin with TW, like "twice" and "twenty" that involve the number 2. But the other two are confused all the time. Just remember that the only meanings of *too* are "also" ("I want some ice cream too") and "in excess" ("Your walkman is playing too loudly.") Note that extra "o." *To* is the proper spelling for all the other uses.

Tortuous / Torturous

Tortuous means full of twists and turns. *Torturous* means "causing or involving torture or suffering." These words are sometimes confused because of their similar spelling, but there is no further similarity.

> **"There are some people who, if they don't already know, you can't tell 'em."**
>
> Yogi Berra

Troop / Troupe

A group of performers is a *troupe*. Any other group of people, military or otherwise, is a *troop*.

Turbid / Turgid

Turbid means "unclear, obscure, confused, disordered" and, when referring to liquids, "muddy, thick, unclear." *Turgid* means "enlarged, swollen" and, when referring to language, "pompous, overblown, grandiloquent."

Commonly Confused Words

Various / Several

Many people say "She heard from various of the committee members that they wanted to cancel the next meeting." *Several* of the committee members would be better.

Vary / Very

Vary means "to change." Don't substitute it for *very* in phrases like "very nice" or "very happy."

Venal / Venial

Venal is an adjective that means corruptible; *venial* is an adjective that means a slight flaw or offense: "In the Catholic church, a venial sin is one that is minor and pardonable, whereas a mortal sin is a serious transgression involving more venal or depraved behavior."

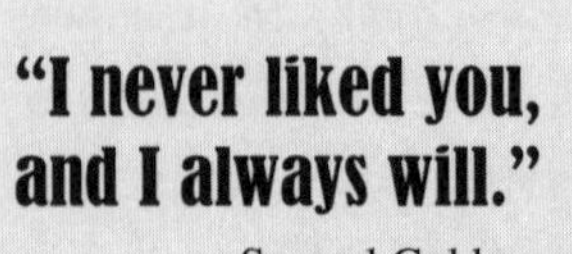

"I never liked you, and I always will."
Samuel Goldwyn

Verses / Versus

The *vs.* in a law case like "Brown vs. The Board of Education" stands for Latin versus (meaning "against"). Don't confuse it with the word for lines of poetry (verses) when describing other conflicts, like the upcoming football game featuring Oakesdale versus Pinewood.

Wary / Weary

People sometimes write *weary* (tired) when they mean *wary* (cautious).

Went / Gone

The past participle of "go" is *gone* so it's not "I should have went to the party" but "I should have gone to the party."

Commonly Confused Words

Who / Whom

The distinction between *who* and *whom* is simple: *who* is the subject form of this pronoun and *whom* is the object form. "Who was wearing that awful dress at the Academy Awards banquet?" is correct because *who* is the subject of the sentence. "The MC was so startled by the neckline that he forgot to whom he was supposed to give the Oscar" is correct because *whom* is the object of the preposition "to." A common hyper-urbanism (or overcorrection) is when someone says, "Whom shall I say is calling?" This is incorrect, but people hear "educated" people say it and repeat it thinking it's correct. There is no object, so it's just "Who shall I say is calling?" or better yet, "Who is calling?"

Who's / Whose

Who's is the contraction of who is. *Whose* is the possessive form of who. "Who's going to figure out whose turn it is to do the dishes?"

Your / You're

Your is the possessive form of you; *you're* is the contraction you are. "If you're planning on swimming, then be sure to bring your life vest and flippers."

Misused Words and Phrases

Misused Words and Phrases

Some words and phrases are not confused with others, they are simply misused themselves. Here are some frequent casualties.

Ain't

Ain't has a long and vital history as a substitute for "isn't," "aren't," and so on. It was originally formed from a contraction of "am not" and is still commonly used in that sense. It's okay to use it occasionally as part of a joking phrase or to convey a down-to-earth quality, but other than that it shouldn't be used.

Allegory

An *allegory* is a narrative in which characters may stand for abstract ideas, and the story convey a philosophy.

Analogy

Students often misuse the word *analogy* in the same way as allegory. An analogy has to be specifically spelled out by the writer, not simply referred to: "My mother's attempts to find her keys in the morning were like early expeditions to the South Pole: prolonged and mostly futile."

Anyways / Anyway / Any how

Anyways, *anyway*, and *any how* (or *anyhow*) should not be used in the following manner: "And anyway, I told you it was going to rain." Or, "Even though I told you it was going to rain, you left your umbrella any how." It is correct to say, "Is there any way you can pick up some milk on your way home?"

As per

As per is a term used in the business world, and Webster defines it as meaning "in accordance with." However, the "as" is unnecessary. "As per your instructions..." sounds pretentious, and should read, "Per your instructions..."

At

Where is Mary at? Behind the *at*. The correct sentence is "Where is Mary?"

"This is unparalyzed in the state's history."

Gib Lewis, Texas speaker of the House

A ways / A way

In some dialects it's common to say "You've got a ways to go before you've saved enough to buy a Miata," but in standard English it's *a way to go*.

A whole 'nother / A completely different

It is one thing to use the expression *a whole 'nother* as a consciously slang phrase suggesting rustic charm and a completely different matter to use it mistakenly. The "a" at the beginning of the phrase is the common article "a" but is here treated as if it were simultaneously the first letter of "another," interrupted by "whole."

Brang / Brung / Brought

In some dialects the past tense of "bring" is *brang* and *brung* is the past participle. In standard English, however, both are *brought*.

Build off of / Build on

You build *on* your earlier achievements, you don't build *off of* them.

Concerted effort

One cannot make a *concerted effort* all by one's self. To work "in concert" is to work together with others.

Conflicted / Conflicted feelings

Phrases like *conflicted feelings* or *I feel conflicted* are considered jargon by many, and out of place in formal writing. Use "I have conflicting feelings" instead, or write "I feel ambivalent."

> **"Things are more like they are now than they ever were before."**
>
> Former President Dwight D. Eisenhower

Contrasts / Contrasts with

With must not be omitted in sentences like this: "Julia's enthusiasm for rugby contrasts with Cheryl's devotion to chess."

Couldn't care less / Could care less

I could care less is incorrect. If you *could care less*, then you care. This term that is meant to convey that one doesn't care, implies "I care so little that I could not care less."

Couple / Couple of

Instead of "They left a couple hours early," write *a couple of hours* if you are trying to sound a bit more formal. Leaving the *of* out is a casual, slangy pattern.

Crank

We no longer *crank* cars, we start them.

Criticism

Beginning literature or art history students are often surprised to learn that in such contexts *criticism* can be a neutral, not negative, term meaning simply "evaluating a work of literature or art." Movie critics write about films they like as well as about films they dislike: writing of both kinds is called *criticism.*

Cut off / Turn Off

Cut off is often used when *turn off* is the appropriate phrase. An example would be, "I'm goin' to bed, will you cut off the light (or television)?" The correct usage is "Will you please turn off the light?"

Deep-seeded / Deep-seated

The expression has nothing to do with a feeling being planted deep within one, but instead refers to its being seated firmly within one's breast: "My aversion to anchovies is deep-seated."

Déjà vu

This usually refers to something excessively familiar. If you feel strongly that you have been previously in a place where you know for a fact you have never before been, you are experiencing a sensation of *déjà vu.*

Depends / Depends on

In casual speech, we say "It depends who plays the best defense"; but in writing follow *depends* with *on.*

Different than / Different from/to

Americans say "Scuba-diving is different from snorkeling"; the British sometimes say *different to* and some people even say *different to. From* is normally preferred.

Misused Words and Phrases

Dire straights / Dire straits

When you are threading your way through troubles as if you were traversing a dangerously narrow passage you are in *dire straits.* The expression and the band by that name are often transformed by those who don't understand the word *strait* into *dire straights.*

Disrespect

The hip-hop subculture has revived the use of *disrespect* as a verb. In the meaning "to have or show disrespect," this usage has been long established. New street usage simply shortens this to "dis."

Drank / Drunk

Many common verbs in English change form when their past tense is preceded by an auxiliary ("helping") verb: "I ran, I have run." The same is true of *drink*. Don't say "I've drank the beer" unless you want people to think you are *drunk*. An even more common error is "I drunk all the milk." It's "I've drunk the beer" and "I drank all the milk."

Drastic

Drastic means "severe" and is always negative. Drastic measures are not just extreme, they are likely to have harmful side-effects. Often people mean "dramatic" instead.

Draw up

Draw up is sometimes used when the speaker means "shrink." "If you wash that shirt in hot water, it will shrink (not draw up)."

Either

Either often gets misplaced in a sentence: "He either wanted to build a gambling casino or a convent" should be "He wanted to build either a gambling casino or a convent." Put *either* just before the first thing being compared.

Misused Words and Phrases

Enthuse

Enthuse is a handy word, but it is not acceptable in the most formal contexts.

Evidence to / Evidence of

You can provide *evidence to* a court, even enough evidence to convict someone; but the standard expression "is *evidence of*" requires *of* rather than *to* in sentences like this: "Driving through the front entrance of the Burger King is evidence of Todd's inexperience in driving."

Feeling bad

"I feel bad" is standard English, as in "This t-shirt smells bad" (not "badly"). "I feel badly" is an over-correction used by some people. People who are happy can correctly say they feel good, but if they say they feel well, we know they mean to say they're healthy.

> **"It is beyond my apprehension."**
>
> Danny Ozark, baseball team manager

Fixing (or fixin' and even fissin')

When people say they are *fixing to* do something, they mean they are getting ready to: "I'm fixing to go to the store." This should correctly be, "I'm getting ready to go to the store."

Flesh out / Flush out

To *flesh out* an idea is to give it substance, as a sculptor adds clay flesh to a skeletal armature. To *flush out* a criminal is to drive him or her out into the open.

For all intensive purposes / For all intents and purposes

For all intents and purposes is cliché, but the correct form of this phrase.

For sale / On sale

If you're selling something, it's *for sale*; but if you lower the price, it goes *on sale*.

> **"The Internet is a gateway to get on the net."**
>
> Former Senate Majority Leader Bob Dole

Fulsome

Because its most common use is in the phrase "fulsome praise," many people suppose that this word means something like "generous" or "whole-hearted." Actually, it means "disgusting," and "fulsome praise" is disgustingly exaggerated praise.

Goes

Goes is often mistakenly used for "says": "So he goes ' I thought your birthday was tomorrow,' and I'm—like—" well, duh!" A deliberate effort should be made to avoid this.

Gotten

In this country, *gotten* is still considered interchangeable with "got" as the past participle of "get," but *got* is preferred except in terms such as "ill-gotten gains."

Graduate / Graduate from

In certain dialects (notably that of New York City) it is common to say "He is going to *graduate* school in June" rather than the more standard *graduate from*. When writing for a national or international audience, use the *from*.

Ground Zero
Ground Zero refers to the point at the center of the impact of a nuclear bomb, so it is improper to talk about "building from ground zero" as if it were a place of new beginnings. You can start from scratch, or begin at zero, but if you're at ground zero, you're at the end. The extension of this term to the site of the destruction of the World Trade Center towers is legitimate.

Grow
We used to *grow* our hair long or grow tomatoes in the yard, but now we are being urged to "grow the economy" or "grow your investments." Business and government speakers have extended this usage widely, but it irritates traditionalists. Use "build," "increase," "expand," "develop," or "cause to grow" instead in formal writing.

Gyp / Cheat
Gypsies complain that *gyp* ("cheat") reflects bias; but the word is so well entrenched that it may not be eliminated from standard use any time soon.

Hardly
Hardly means "with difficulty." Using this word along usually does not create a problem, but often it is used with "can't," which creates a double negative. When Bill says "I can't hardly bend over with this backache," he means he can hardly bend over, and that's what he should say.

Hisself / Himself
In some dialects people say *hisself* for *himself*, but this is nonstandard.

Hoi Polloi

Hoi polloi is Greek for "the common people," but it is often misused to mean "the upper class" (does "hoi" make speakers think of "high" or "hoity-toity"?). Some urge that since *hoi* is the article the *hoi polloi* is redundant; but it is considered to be standard English.

Hold your peace / Say your piece

These sound similar, but are unrelated. *Hold your peace* means "to maintain your silence." *Say your piece* means literally "speak aloud a piece of writing" but is used to express the idea of making a statement.

Home in / Hone in

You *home in* (focus on) a target. *Honing* has to do with sharpening knives, not aim.

Home page

On the World Wide Web, a *home page* is normally the first page a person entering a site encounters, often functioning as a sort of table of contents for the other pages. People sometimes create special pages within their sites introducing a particular topic, and these are also informally called *home pages*.

Homophobic

Some object to this word, arguing that it literally means "man-fearing," but it is now an established term for "prejudiced against homosexuals."

Hose pipe

When people refer to a *hose pipe*, they usually mean only the hose. The hose pipe is the pipe that the hose connects to.

How come / Why

How come? is a common question in casual speech, but in formal contexts use *"Why?"*

Hypocritical

Hypocritical has a narrow, very specific meaning. It describes behavior or speech that is intended to make one look better or more pious than one really is. It is often wrongly used to label people who are merely narrow-minded or genuinely pious. Do not confuse this word with "hypercritical," which describes people who are picky.

If I was / If I were

The subjunctive mood, always weak in English, has been dwindling away for centuries until it has almost vanished. However, one modern distinction is this: Use *if I was* when you are talking about something that actually happened. "If I was rude just now, I apologize." Use *if I were* for hypothetical statements: "If I were rich, I would go to Paris."

> **"It's no exaggeration to say that the undecideds could go one way or another."**
>
> Former President George H. Bush

Impact

Impact has come to be used as a verb, meaning "to influence" : "This news will impact the price of gasoline."As a noun, it means "an effect": "The effect will be felt immediately."

Incredible

Incredible literally means "unbelievable," but this and other intensifiers and superlatives tend to get diluted through overuse, and have become almost meaningless. To preserve their significance, they should be used sparingly.

Infinite

Infinite means limitless or boundless, without beginning or end. It is sometimes grouped with other absolute terms like *unique*, because there are no degrees of infinity. Words like *nearly* and *almost* should not be used with infinite.

Inflammable

Inflammable means the same thing as "flammable": burnable, capable of being ignited or inflamed. Because so many people mistake the "in-" prefix as a negative, it has been largely abandoned as a warning label.

> **"She's really tough; she's remorseful."**
>
> David Moorcroft

Input

Input, something that is "put in," began as computer jargon and has proliferated in the business world. Be careful not to use this as "imput."

In regards to / With regard to

"With regards to your downsizing plan . . ." is acceptable, if stiff. "In regard to . . ." is also correct. But don't confuse the two by writing "In regards to."

Intensifiers

Intensifiers are simply words that boost descriptions. People are always looking for ways to emphasize how special the subject under discussion is. Words like "really" and "very" are worn thin from overuse. When you are tempted to use one of these vague intensifiers consider rephrasing to explain more precisely and vividly what you mean: "Fred's cooking was incredibly bad" could be changed to "When I tasted Fred's cooking I almost thought I was back in the middle-school cafeteria."

Misused Words and Phrases

In the fact that / In that

Many people mistakenly write *in the fact that* when they mean simply *in that* in sentences like "It seemed wiser not to go to work in the fact that the boss had discovered the company picnic money was missing." Omit "the fact." Also note that infact is not a word; *in fact* is always a two-word phrase.

Intrigue

Something mysterious or alluring can be called *intriguing*, but *intrigue* as a noun means a secret scheme or plot. Don't say people or situations are full of *intrigue* when you mean they are intriguing.

Is, is

In speech, people often lose track in the middle of a sentence and repeat *is* instead of saying "that": "The problem with the conflict in the Balkans is, is the ethnic tensions seem exacerbated by everything we do." This is a nervous tic to avoid when speaking publicly.

It / there

It is often used in spoken language to mean *there*. For example, "It is a lot of people at the concert," should be "There are a lot of people at the concert."

Like

The habit of including *like* as an extraneous word in verbal communication has been called "a verbal hiccup." It is inserted randomly in conversation: "I went, like, crazy." It is annoying to listen to in casual conversation, but in professional circles, can undermine a polished image.

Literally

Literally (meaning "actually") has been so overused as an intensifier that it is in danger of losing its meaning. It should be used to distinguish between a figurative and a literal meaning of a phrase. It should not be used as a synonym for "actually" or "really."

Lived

In expressions like "long-lived" pronouncing *lived* to rhyme with "dived" is more traditional, but rhyming it with "sieved" is so common that it's now widely acceptable.

Mash

Don't say *mash* when you mean press. To *mash* is to crush. To *press* means simply to apply pressure. So when you say, "Will you please mash the button for the 4th floor?" you really mean, "Will you please press the button?"

> **"A low voter turnout is an indication of fewer people going to the polls."**
>
> Former Vice President Al Gore

Median

That strip of grass separating the lanes going opposite directions in the middle of a freeway is a *median*, not a medium.

Mediocre

Although some dictionaries accept the meaning of this word as "medium" or "average," in fact its connotations are almost always more negative. When something is distinctly not as good as it could be, it is *mediocre*.

Might could

You *might* pick up a loaf of bread at the store or you *could* pick up a loaf of bread at the store. Pick only one.

Misused Words and Phrases

Misnomer

A *misnomer* is a mistake in naming a thing, such as when we call a debit card a "credit card." Do not use the term to indicate other sorts of confusion, misunderstood concepts, or fallacies, and above all do not express this word as "misnamer."

More importantly / More important

When speakers are trying to impress audiences with their rhetoric, they often seem to feel that the extra syllable in *importantly* lends weight to their remarks: "And more importantly, I have an abiding love for the American people." However, these pompous speakers are wrong. It is rarely correct to use this form of the phrase because it is seldom adverbial in intention. Say *more important* instead. The same applies to *most importantly*; it should be *most important*.

Most always / Almost always

Most always is a casual, slangy way of saying *almost always*. The latter expression is better in writing.

Much differently / Very differently

Say "We consistently vote *very differently*," not *much differently*. But you can say "My opinion doesn't much differ from yours."

Mute point / Moot point

Moot is a very old word related to "meeting," specifically a meeting where serious matters are discussed. Oddly enough, a moot point can be a point worth discussing at a meeting, or it can be the opposite: a point already settled and not worth discussing further. At any rate, *mute point* is simply wrong.

Nonplussed

Nonplussed means to be stuck, often in a puzzling or embarrassing way, unable to go further. Many people erroneously think it means "calm, in control."

No sooner when / No sooner than
The phrase, "No sooner had Paula stopped petting the cat when it began to yowl" should be instead, "No sooner had Paula stopped petting the cat than it began to yowl."

Old fashion / Old-fashioned
Although *old fashion* appears in advertising a good deal, the traditional spelling is *old-fashioned.*

Old-timer's Disease / Alzheimer's Disease
Old-timer's Disease is an often used, but incorrect, name for *Alzheimer's Disease.*

On accident / By accident
Although you can do things on purpose, you do them *by accident.*

Once and a while / Once in a while
The correct expression is *once in a while.*

Only
Writers often inadvertently create confusion by placing *only* incorrectly in a sentence. It should go immediately before the word or phrase it modifies. "I lost my only shirt" means that I had but one to begin with. "I lost only my shirt" means I didn't lose anything else. "Only I lost my shirt" means that I was the only person in my group to lose a shirt.

Orientate
Although some dictionaries have now begun to accept it, *orientate* was mistakenly formed from *orientation*. The proper verb form is simply *orient*. Similarly, "disorientated" is an error for "disoriented."

Palm off / Pawn off
Somebody defrauds you by using sleight of hand (literal or figurative) to *palm* the object you wanted and give you something inferior instead. The expression is not *to pawn off*, but *to palm off.*

Misused Words and Phrases

Per / According to

Using *per* to mean *according to* as in "ship the widgets as per the instructions of the customer" is rather old-fashioned business jargon, and is not welcome in other contexts. *Per* is fine when used in phrases involving figures like "miles per gallon."

Phenomena / Phenomenon

These are two of several words with Latin or Greek roots whose plural forms ending in "a" are constantly mistaken for singular ones. It's *this phenomenon* (singular), but *these phenomena* (plural).

Playwrite / Playwright

It might seem as if a person who writes plays should be called a *playwrite;* but in fact a *playwright* is a person who has wrought words into a dramatic form, just as a wheelwright has wrought wheels out of wood and iron.

Plead innocent

Lawyers frown on the phrase *plead innocent.* (It's "plead guilty" or "plead not guilty"); but outside of legal contexts the phrase is standard English.

> **"A verbal contract isn't worth the paper it's written on."**
>
> Samuel Goldwyn

Possessed of / Possessed by / Possessed with

If you own a yacht, you're *possessed of it.* If a demon takes over your body, you're *possessed by it.* If that which possesses you is more metaphorical, like an executive determined to get ahead, he or she can be *possessed by or with* the desire to win.

Prejudice / Prejudiced

People not only misspell *prejudice* in a number of ways, they sometimes say "He's prejudice" when they mean "He's prejudiced."

Quote

A passage doesn't become a *quote* (or a quotation) until you've quoted it. The only time to refer to a *quote* is when you are referring to someone quoting something. When referring to the original words, simply call it a passage.

Ratio

A *ratio* is a way of expressing the relationship between one number and another. If there is one teacher to fifty students, the teacher/student ratio is one to fifty, and the student/teacher ratio fifty to one. If a very dense but wealthy prince were being tutored by fifty teachers, the teacher/student ratio would be fifty to one, and the student/teacher ratio would be one to fifty. As you can see, the order in which the numbers are compared is important.

> **"Excuse me for not answering your letter sooner, but I've been so busy not answering letters that I couldn't get around to not answering yours in time."**
>
> Groucho Marx

Reeking havoc / Wreaking havoc

Reeking means "smelling strongly," so that can't be right. The phrase simply means "working great destruction." *Havoc* has always referred to general destruction in English, but one very old phrase incorporating the word was "cry havoc," which meant to give an army the signal for pillage.

Misused Words and Phrases

Remotely close

"Not even remotely close" is a fine example of an oxymoron. An idea can be "not even remotely correct," but closeness and remoteness are opposites; it doesn't make sense to have one modify the other.

Religion believes / Religion teaches

People often write things like "Buddhism believes" when they mean to say "Buddhism teaches," or "Buddhists believe." Religions do not believe, they are the objects of belief.

Right of passage / Rite of passage

The more common phrase is *rite of passage*, a ritual one goes through to move on to the next stage of life. Learning how to work the combination on a locker is a rite of passage for many entering middle school students. A *right of passage* would be the right to travel through a certain territory, but you are unlikely to have any use for the phrase.

Row to hoe / Road to hoe

Out in the cotton patch you have a tough *row to hoe*. This saying has nothing to do with road construction, so *road to hoe* is improper.

Safety deposit box / Safe-deposit box

"Safety" is rarely pronounced very differently from "safe-D" so it is natural that many people suppose they are hearing the word at the beginning of this phrase, but the correct expression is in fact *safe-deposit box.*

Second of all / Second

"First of all" makes sense when you want to emphasize the primacy of the first item in a series, but it should not be followed by *second of all* where the expression serves no such function. As you go through your list, say simply "second," "third," "fourth," etc.

Setup / Set up

Technical writers sometimes confuse *setup* as a noun ("check the setup") with the phrase *set up* ("set up the experiment").

Simplistic

Simplistic means "overly simple," and is always used negatively. Don't substitute it when you just mean to say "simple" or even "very simple."

Slight of hand / Sleight of hand

Sleight is an old word meaning "cleverness, skill," and the proper expression is *sleight of hand.* It's easy to understand why it's confused with "slight" since the two words are pronounced in exactly the same way.

Sometime / Some time

"Let's get together sometime." When you use the one-word form, it suggests some indefinite time in the future. *Some time* is not wrong in this sort of context, but it is required when being more specific: "Choose some time that fits in your schedule." *Some* is an adjective here modifying "time." The same pattern applies to "someday" (vague) and "some day" (specific).

Sour grapes

In a famous fable by Aesop, a fox declared that he didn't care that he could not reach an attractive bunch of grapes because he imagined they were probably sour anyway. You express *sour grapes* when you talk negatively about something you can't get: "Winning the lottery is just a big headache anyway." The phrase is misused in all sorts of ways by people who don't know the original story and imagine it means something more general like "bitterness" or "resentment."

Spitting image

Spit and image is the correct form for this crude figure of speech implying that someone else is enough like you to have been spat out by you, made of the very stuff of your body. In the early 20th century the spelling and pronunciation gradually shifted to the less logical "spitting image," which is now standard. There is no historical basis for the claim sometimes made that the original expression was "spirit and image."

Substance-free

An administrator at a university announced recently that his goal was a *substance-free* campus, which I suppose fits in with the growing fad of "virtual education." What he really meant was, of course, a campus free of illegal drugs and alcohol, designated "controlled substances" in the law.

> **"It's tough to make predictions, especially about the future."**
>
> Yogi Berra

Substitute for / Substitute with

You can *substitute* pecans *for* the walnuts in a brownie recipe, but many people mistakenly say *substitute with* instead, perhaps influenced by the related expression "replace with." It's always *substitute for.*

Suffer with / Suffer from

Although technical medical usage sometimes differs, in normal speech we say that a person *suffers from* a disease rather than *suffering with* it.

Supposably or supposingly / Supposedly

Supposedly is the standard form for these very similar words.

Suppose to / Supposed to

Because the "d" and the "t" are blended into a single consonant when this phrase is pronounced, many writers are unaware that the "d" is even present and omit it in writing.

> **"I'm not going to have some reporters pawing through our papers. We are the President."**
>
> Hillary Clinton

Take a different tact / Take a different tack

This expression has nothing to do with tactfulness and everything to do with sailing, in which it is a direction taken as one *tacks* (abruptly turns) a boat. To *take a different tack* is to try another approach.

Taken back / Taken aback

When you're startled by something, you're *taken aback* by it. When you're reminded of something from your past, you're *taken back* to that time.

That kind / That kind of

Although expressions like *that kind thing* are common in some dialects, standard English requires *of* in this kind of phrase.

These are them / These are they

Although only the pickiest listeners will cringe when you say "*These are them,*" the traditionally correct phrase is "*These are they.* " However, if people around you seem more comfortable with "It's me" than "It's I," you might as well stick with "These are them."

These kind / This kind

Use *these* when the word *kind* is plural. Use *this* when *kind* is singular.

Though / Thought / Through

Though means "nevertheless." *Thought* is "the act of thinking." And *through* indicates movement in one side and out another. These words have very different meanings, and most people know those, but often type one of them when they mean another. Spelling checkers won't catch this sort of slip, so look out for it.

To home / At home

In some dialects people say "I stayed *to home* to wait for the mail," but in standard English the expression is stayed *at home.*

Tolled / Told

Some people imagine that the expression should be "all tolled" as if items were being ticked off to the tolling of a bell, or involved the paying of a toll; but in fact this goes back to an old meaning of "tell": "to count." You could "tell over" your beads if you were counting them in a rosary. *All told* means "all counted."

Tongue and cheek / Tongue in cheek

When people want to show they are kidding or have just knowingly uttered a falsehood, they stick their tongues in their cheeks, so it's *tongue in cheek*, not *tongue and cheek.*

Use to / Used to

Because the "d" and the "t" are blended into a single consonant when this phrase is pronounced, many writers are unaware that the "d" is even present and omit it in writing. However, the proper usage is *used to.*

Vale of tears / Veil of tears

The expression *vale of tears* goes back to pious sentiments that consider life on earth to be a series of sorrows to be left behind when we go on to a better world in Heaven. It conjures up an image of a suffering traveler laboring through a valley ("vale") of troubles and sorrow. While *veil of tears* may sound poetic, it is incorrect.

Very unique / Unique

Unique indicates one of a kind. A thing is unique or it is not; there are no degrees of being unique so nothing is *very unique.*

Vicious circle / Vicious cycle

Although both forms of this figure of speech would seem to be accurate, the *vicious circle* is actually the correct term.

Wet your appetite / Whet your appetite

It is natural to think that something mouth-watering *wets your appetite,* but actually the expression is *whet your appetite,* as a whetstone sharpens a knife.

Whether / Whether or not

Whether works fine on its own in most contexts: "I wonder whether I forgot to turn off the stove?" But when you mean "regardless of whether" it has to be followed by "or not" somewhere in the sentence: "We need to leave for the airport in five minutes whether you've found your teddy bear or not."

Commonly Misspelled Words

Commonly Misspelled Words

Here is a quick reference for correct spelling of words that are often troublesome.

a lot NOT: alot
a while NOT: awhile
absence
abundance
accelerate
accessible
accidentally NOT: accidently
acclaim
accommodate NOT: accomodate
accomplish
accordion NOT: accordian
accumulate
achievement
acquaintance NOT: acquaintence, aquaintance
acquire NOT: aquire
acquit NOT: aquit
address
advertisement
advice
advise
affidavit NOT: affidavid
after all NOT: afterall
aggravate
alleged
amateur
analysis
analyze
anchors aweigh NOT: anchors away
anoint NOT annoint
anticlimactic NOT: anticlimatic
apology
apparatus
apparent
appearance
Arabic numbers Not: Aerobic numbers
arctic NOT: artic
argument NOT: arguement
arithmetic
article NOT: artical
ascend
asphalt NOT: ashfault
asterisk NOT: asterick
atheist
athletic
attendance
auxiliary
axle NOT: axel
balloon
barbecue NOT: barbeque
bargain
basically

Commonly Misspelled Words

bated breath NOT: baited breath
battalion NOT: batallion
beggar
beginning
belief
believable NOT: believeable
believe
beneficial
benefited
blessing in disguise NOT: blessing in the sky
biscuit
boatload NOT: buttload
boon to the economy NOT: boom to the economy
boundaries NOT: boundries
bouillon
bound NOT: binded
brand new NOT: bran new
Britain NOT: Britin
broccoli NOT: brocolli
business
buttocks NOT: buttox
Caesar NOT: Ceasar
calendar NOT: calender
cardsharp NOT: cardshark
case in point NOT: case and point
catalytic converter NOT: Cadillac converter
camouflage NOT: camoflage
candidate
cantaloupe
carburetor
Caribbean
cartilage
category
cemetery NOT: cemetary
champ at the bit NOT: chomp at the bit
changeable
changing
chauvinism NOT: chauvanism
chicken pox NOT: chicken pops
chock full NOT: chalk full
choose
chose
circumcised NOT: circus sized
clarified NOT: clearified
coliseum NOT: colliseum or colosseum
collectible NOT: collectable
colonel
commemorate
commission
committee
comparative
compelled
competent
completely

concede
conceivable
conceive
condemn
condescend
conferred
congratulations NOT: congradulated
conscience
conscientious
conscious
consciousness
consensus NOT: concensus
consistent
continuous
controlled
controversial
controversy
convenient
converse NOT: conversate
correlate
cornet NOT: coronet
coolly NOT cooly
copyright NOT: copywrite
copyrighted NOT: copywritten
corollary
correspondence
cortege NOT: cortage
coup de grace NOT: coup de gras
counselor
courteous
courtesy
crème de menthe NOT: cream de mint
criticize
crucified NOT: crossified
crucifixion NOT: crucifiction
cul de sac NOT: culvert sack
cummerbund NOT: cumberbun
daiquiri
Dalmatian NOT: Dalmation
deceive
defendant
deferred
definite NOT: definate
definitely NOT: definitely
déjà vu NOT: deja vous
dependent
desiccate NOT: dessicate
despair NOT: dispair
desperate NOT: desparate
deterrence
develop
development NOT: developement
dictionary
difference
definite
dilate NOT: dialate
dilemma
diorama

Commonly Misspelled Words

disappear
disappearance
disappoint
disastrous
discipline
disease
dispensable
dissatisfied
dissipate NOT: disippate
distraught NOT: diswraught
documented NOT: documentated
dog-eat-dog world NOT: doggy dog world
dominant
dormitory
down the pike NOT: down the pipe
drowned NOT: drownded
drowning NOT: drownding
drunkenness NOT: drunkeness
dumbbell NOT: dumbell
ecstasy NOT: ecstacy
effect
efficiency
eighth
either
electoral college NOT: electorial college
eligible
eliminate
embarrass
embarrassment NOT: embarassment
embedded NOT: imbedded
eminent
encouragement
encouraging
en masse NOT: in mass
entirely
environment
equipped
escape NOT: excape
especially NOT: expecially
every day NOT: everyday
every time NOT: everytime
exacting revenge NOT: extracting revenge
exaggerate
exceed NOT: excede
excellence
exercise NOT: excercise
exhilaration
existence NOT: existance
existent
exorbitant price NOT: exuberant price
expatriate NOT: ex-patriot
expense
experience
experiment
explanation

Commonly Misspelled Words

extremely
exuberance
Fahrenheit
fair to middling NOT: fair to midland
fallacious
fallacy
false sense of security NOT: sense of false security
familiar
fascinate
February
fell swoop NOT: foul swoop
fictitious
final throes NOT: final throws
financially
fiery NOT: firey
flabbergast NOT: flabberghast
florescent
flotation NOT: floatation
foliage NOT: foilage
forcibly
foreign
foresee
forfeit
formerly
forty NOT: fourty
frantically
frustrated NOT: flustrated
frustum NOT: frustrum
fulfill
fundamentally
Gandhi NOT: Ghandi
gauge
genera NOT: genuses
generally
genius NOT: genious; as in "ingenious"
genre NOT: jaundra
glean NOT: gleam
government
governor
grammar NOT: grammer
grandeur
grateful NOT: greatful
grievous
guarantee
guard NOT: gaurd
guerrilla
guidance
guttural
handkerchief NOT: hankerchief
harass NOT: harrass harbinger NOT: harbringer
harebrained NOT: hairbrained
harm's way NOT: arm's way
heard NOT: heared
heart – rending NOT: heart-rendering
height NOT: heighth
Heimlich maneuver NOT: Heineken remover

Commonly Misspelled Words

heinous
hemorrhage
heroes
hesitancy
hierarchy
hindrance NOT hinderance
hoarse
hobbyist NOT: hobbiest
hoping
horrific
humorous
hypocrisy NOT: hyprocracy
hypocrite
iced tea NOT: ice tea
ideally
idiosyncrasy
ignorance
imaginary
immediately
impending doom NOT: impaling doom
implement
inadvertent NOT: inadvertant
incidentally NOT: incidently
incredible
independence
independent NOT: independent
in-depth NOT: indepth
indicted
indispensable NOT: indispensible
inevitable
in fact NOT: infact
influential
information
ingenious NOT: ingenius; see "genius"
in light of NOT: in lieu of
inoculate NOT: innoculate
insinuation or innuendo NOT: insinnuendo
insistent NOT: insistant
insurmountable NOT: insuremountable
in synch NOT: in sink
intact NOT: in tact
integral NOT: intragul
intellectual
intelligence
intercede
interesting
interference
interpret NOT: interpretate
interrupt
in the same vein NOT: in the same vane or vain
irascible
irrelevant
irresistible NOT: irresistable
irritable NOT: irritible
Isaac NOT: Issac
island

ivory tower NOT: ivy tower
jealousy
judgment NOT: judgement
judicial
just as soon NOT: just assume
knowledge
Ku Klux Klan NOT: Klu Klux Klan
lackadaisical NOT: lacksadaisical
lambasted NOT: lamblasted, landblasted
larynx NOT: larnyx
legitimate
leisure
lenient
liaison NOT: liason
license
lieutenant
lightning
likelihood
liquefy NOT: liquify
liquor NOT: likker
lo and behold NOT: low and behold
loneliness
longitude
loosen NOT: unloosen
losing
maintenance
manageable
maneuver
manufacture
marshal NOT: marshall
marshmallow NOT: marshmellow
mashed potatoes NOT: smashed potatoes
masonry NOT: masonary
mathematics
maybe
meantime NOT: mean time
medicine
medieval, also mediaeval
memento NOT: momento
memoriam NOT: memorium
menstruate NOT: menestrate
mere
mete out justice NOT: meter out justice
militate against NOT: mitigate against
millennium NOT: millenium
millionaire
miniature
minuscule NOT: miniscule
mischief NOT: mischeif
mischievous NOT: mischievio
misconstrue NOT: misconscrewus
misogyny

Commonly Misspelled Words

mispronunciation NOT: mispronounciation
missile NOT: misile
misspell NOT: mispell
more so NOT: moreso
mortgage
mosquito
mosquitoes
mural NOT: muriel
myocardial infarction NOT: myocardial infraction
mysterious
naive
narrative
necessary
necessity
neck and neck NOT: neck in neck
new lease on life NOT: new leash on life
neighbor
neutron
niece NOT: neice
ninth
ninety
no one NOT: noone
notary public NOT: notary republic
noticeable
nowadays
nuisance
nuptial NOT: nupital
obedience
objet d'art NOT: oject d'art
obstacle
occasion NOT: ocassion
occasionally
occurred
occurrence NOT: ocurrence or occur
octopus NOT: octopus
odoriferous NOT: odiferousrence
offense NOT: offence
official
omission
omitted NOT: ommitted
onomatopoeia
opponent
oppression
ordinarily
ostensibly NOT: ostensively
outrageous
overalls NOT: overhauls
overrun
overzealous NOT: overjealous
painstaking NOT: pain-staking

Commonly Misspelled Words

panicky
parallel
paralleled
paralysis
paralyze
parliament NOT: parlament
part and parcel NOT: part in parcel
pastoral NOT: pastorial
patriarchal NOT: patriarticle
pavilion
peaceable
peculiar
pedestal NOT: pedastool
peninsula
perceive
peripheral NOT: periphial
permanent
permissible
permitted
per se NOT: perse
perseverance
persistence
persnickety NOT: pernickety
perspiration
peruse
pervert NOT: prevert
pharaoh NOT: pharoah
physical
physician
picnicking
piecemeal NOT: peacemeal
pigeon NOT: pidgeon
pilgrimage
pistachio NOT: pistacchio
pitiful
playwright NOT: playright
plenitude NOT: plentitude
poison ivy NOT: poison ivory
poltergeist NOT: poultrygeist
portentous NOT: portentious
portray NOT: protray
potato
potatoes
practically
prairie
precede
precedence
predominantly NOT: predominately
preemptory NOT: peremptory
preference
preferred
prejudice NOT: predjudice
preparation
prerogative NOT: perogative
prescription NOT: perscription
presumably NOT: assumably
presumptuous NOT: presumptious
prevalent: NOT: prevalant

Commonly Misspelled Words

prima donna NOT: pre-Madonna
primitive
privilege NOT: priviledge
probably
procedure
proceed
professor
prominent
promiscuous NOT: permiscuous
pronounce
pronunciation NOT: pronounciation
propaganda
propagate
proverbial NOT: perverbial
prurient interest NOT: Peruvian interest
psychology
publicly
puerile
pumpkin NOT: punkin, pumkin
pursue NOT: persue
putrefy
quandary
quantity
quarantine
questionnaire
quizzes
rabble rouser NOT: rebel rouser
radical chic NOT: radical chick
rappel NOT: repel
rapport NOT: rapore
raspberry
realistically
recede NOT: receed
receipt
receive NOT: receive
reckless NOT: wreckless
recommend NOT: recommend
recurring NOT: reoccurring
reference
referred
referring
refrigerator NOT: refridgerator
reinvent the wheel NOT: recreate the wheel
relevant
relieving
religious
remembrance
reminiscence
renowned
repetition NOT: repitition
representative
resemblance
reservoir
restaurant

Commonly Misspelled Words

retroactive increase NOT: radioactive increase
rheumatism
rhyme
rhythm
rhythmical
ridiculous
roommate
sacrifice
sacrilegious NOT: sacreligious
sandal
satellite
savvy
scapegoat NOT: escape goat
scary
scenery
secede
secretary
seize NOT: sieze
seize the day NOT: cease the day
self-esteem NOT: self of steam
sense
sensible NOT: sensable
sentence
separate NOT: seperate
septuagenarian NOT: septagenarian
sergeant
severely
shepherd
sherbet NOT: sherbert
sheriff
shining
shish kebab
shudder to think NOT: shutter to think
siege
similar NOT: similar or simular
simile
sincerely
six of one, half a dozen of the other NOT: six and a half of one, dozen of the other
skiing
skittish NOT: skiddish
sliver of cake NOT: slither of cake
slough off NOT: sluff off
smoke and mirrors NOT: smoking mirrors
smothered with onions NOT: smothered onions
soliloquy
something or other NOT: something or rather
somnolent NOT: somulent
sophomore
sorcerer NOT: sorceror
sordid past NOT: sorted past
souvenir
spayed NOT: spaded

Commonly Misspelled Words

specific NOT: pacific
specifically
speculation NOT: expeculation
spontaneous
stained glass NOT: stain glass
statistics
statue
stopped
straitjacket NOT: straightjacket
strategy
strenuous
stubbornness
studying
subordinate
subpoena NOT: subpena
subtle
succeed
success
succession
sufficient
supersede NOT: supercede
supposedly NOT: supposably or supposingly
suppress
supremacist NOT: supremist
surreal NOT: sureal
surround
susceptible
suspicious
syllable
symmetrical
synonymous
tangible
tariff
technique
technology NOT: techknowledgy
temperamental
temperature
tendency
tenterhooks NOT: tender hooks
thaw NOT: unthaw
themselves
theories
therefore NOT: therefor
thorough
though
threshold
through
tide me over NOT: tie me over
Tijuana NOT: Tiajuna
toe the line NOT: tow the line
told NOT: tolled
tomorrow
tongue
took it for granted NOT: took it for granite
tournament
tourniquet
tragedy NOT: tradgedy
transferred
transferring

tries
turpentine NOT: turpentime
twelfth
tyrannical yoke NOT: tyrannical yolk
tyranny NOT: tyrrany
ukulele NOT: ukelele
unanimous
uncharted territory NOT: unchartered territory
unconscious NOT: unconscience
undoubtedly
unnecessary
usage
usually
vacuum
Valentines NOT: Valentimes
vengeance
verbiage NOT: verbage
viaduct NOT: viadock
vice versa NOT: visa versa
vicious
vigilant
village
villain
vinaigrette NOT: vinegarette
violence
vocal cords NOT: vocal chords
vulnerable NOT: vunerable
warrant
Wednesday
weird NOT: weird
welt NOT: whelp
wherever
which NOT: witch
whisky
wholly
Wimbledon NOT: Wimbleton
wind chill factor NOT: windshield factor
without further ado NOT: without further adieu
wolf in sheep's clothing NOT: wolf in cheap clothing
world-renowned NOT:
world-renown
worst-case scenario NOT: worse case scenario
worth its salt/worth its weight in gold NOT: worth its weight in salt
worthwhile NOT: worth wild
wrought iron NOT: rot or rod iron
yacht
yield NOT: yeild
zoology

Redundancies

Redundancies

Redundancies are words that are frequently used together but because their meanings overlap, only one of them is needed.

A.M. in the morning
AC current
ACT test
actual facts
add an additional
add up
added bonus
advance forward
advance planning
advance preview
advance reservations
advance scouting
advance warning
affirmative yes
aid and abet
all-time record
alternative choice
and et cetera
annual anniversary
anonymous stranger
armed gunman
ascend up
ask the question
assemble together
at about
ATM machine
attach together
bald-headed
basic fundamentals
basic necessities
best ever
blend together
boat marine
both together
bouquet of flowers
breaking and entering
brief in duration
brief moment
brief summary
burn down
burning embers
cacophony of sound
cameo appearance
cancel out
careful scrutiny
cash money
cease and desist
circulate around
classic tradition
climb up
close proximity
CNN news
collaborate together
combine together

Redundancies

combined total
commute back and forth
completely destroy
completely eliminate
completely engulf
completely fill
completely surround
component parts
conclusive proof
connect together
connect up
conniption fit
consensus of opinion
continue on
cooperate together
courthouse building
couture fashion
customary practice
dead corpse
depreciate in value
descend down
disappear from sight
doctorate degree
drop down
during the course of
each and every
eliminate altogether
empty hole
enclosed herewith
end result
endorse on the back
enter into
eradicate completely
estimated at about
evolve over time
exact replica
exact same
factual information
fall down
favorable approval
few in number
filled to capacity
final conclusion
final end
final outcome
finished product
first and foremost
first of all
fly through the air
follow after
following below
forced compulsion
foreign imports
frank candor
free gift
French dip with au jus
from whence
frozen ice
frozen tundra
future potential
future recurrence
gather together

Redundancies

GOP party
GRE exam
grow in size
had done previously
harmful injuries
head honcho
HIV virus
illustrated drawing
in this day and age
indicted on a charge
inner core
input into
integrate together
integrate with each other
introduced a new
invited guests
irregardless
ISBN number
join together
joint collaboration
kills bugs dead
kneel down
knowledgeable experts
lag behind
later time
LCD display
lift up
linger on
literate readers
live studio audience
live witness
look ahead to the future
look back in retrospect
made out of
malignant cancer
manually by hand
many frequent
Medieval Ages
mental telepathy
might possibly
missing gaps
mix together
mutual cooperation
mutually interdependent
nape of her neck
native habitat
natural instinct
near proximity
never ever
new beginner
new beginning
new innovation
new neophyte
new recruit
none at all
normal everyday
nostalgia for the past
now pending
null and void
off of
old adage
old custom

Redundancies

old proverb
on account of the fact that
open trench
open up
original prototype
original source
outside in the yard
over again
over exaggerated
overused cliché
pair of twins
palm of the hand
passing fad
past experience
PC computer
penetrate into
perfect circle
period of time
personal belongings
personal friend
personal opinion
pick and choose
PIN number
pizza pie
plan ahead
plan in advance
Please RSVP
plunge down
point being is that
point in time
poisonous venom
polar opposites
postpone until later
pouring down rain
present incumbent
present time
prior history
proceed ahead
proposed plan
protest against
protrude out
pursue after
RAM memory
rarely ever
reason because
reason why
recur again
re-elect for another term
reflect back
regular routine
repeat again
reply back
rest and relaxation
retreat back
return back
revert back
rise up
root cause
round in shape
safe haven
safe sanctuary
salsa sauce

Redundancies

same identical
SAT test
scrutinize in detail
separate apart
serious crisis
shape and form
share together
sharp point
Sierra Nevada Mountains
small minority
small speck
sole of the foot
soup du jour of the day
spliced together
still persists
still remains
sudden impulse
sum total
surround on all sides
tall in height
tall in stature
temper tantrum
temporary reprieve
time period
top priority
total chaos
true fact
truly sincere
tuna fish
two equal halves
two twins
two-man tandem
ultimate goal
underground subway
unexpected surprise
unintentional mistake
up above
UPC code
useless and unnecessary
usual custom
vacillating back and forth
very unique
viable alternative
visible to the eye
wall mural
warn in advance
water hydrant
whether or not
whole entire
widow woman
will and testament
with au jus

Special Usage and Style Problems

Special Usage and Style Problems

Even after thoughts are organized and words are chosen, the mechanics of speaking and writing English offer special problems. Here are just a few that often cause confusion.

Active / Passive voice

When sentences are in the active voice, the subject *does* the action. In passive voice, the subject *receives* the action.

Active: *John left the copier on overnight.*

Passive: *The copier was left on overnight.*

The passive voice has its uses, but the majority of our speaking and writing should be in active voice. It is stronger, has more energy, and is more direct.

> **"We must believe in free will. We have no choice."**
>
> Isaac Bashevis Singer

Colons and Semicolons

Colons have been called "two little dots (like headlights) that indicate that something is coming ahead." They let you know that a quotation, an example, or a list will follow. Sometimes they are used after words like *as follows, such as,* and *the following*:

Diners will request substitutions such as: potatoes, gravy, and rolls.

The article stated the following: "The manager will be held responsible."

Colons should not follow a verb. Note in the following sentence that no colon is needed.

My favorite things include cool weather, falling leaves, and good coffee.

Semicolons are used to separate two complete thoughts that could each stand alone, but are joined because they are related.

My favorite holiday is Thanksgiving; it reminds me to be grateful.

When the second part of a compound sentence begins with a transition word or phrase such as *however, therefore, yet, moreover, as a result, in summary, on the contrary, consequently, for example,* or other similar words, use a semicolon.

The meeting was long; nevertheless, much was accomplished.

No one was surprised by the announcement; in fact, we were expecting it.

Ellipses

Three little dots in a row are called an *ellipsis,* which means to fall short or leave out. The ellipsis indicates that something is being omitted from some part of the sentence.

An ellipsis . . .indicates the omission of words in a sentence.

Her tribute began with the words, "It is my honor to . . . ."

When the ellipsis comes at the end of a sentence, a fourth period is added to serve as the final punctuation for the sentence. Also, style manuals differ about whether spaces should be added between the dots of an ellipsis. Check your particular format requirements for which you should do.

Numbers

The general rule is to spell out in words whole numbers from one through ninety-nine, and to spell out numbers that begin a sentence. Numbers twenty-one through twenty-nine, thirty-one to thirty-nine and so on, are hyphenated. When writing or speaking, numbers are pronounced as follows: 1007 is "one thousand seven." Note it is not "one thousand *and* seven." Therefore, the year is "two thousand four," not "two thousand *and* four." The only time you add *and* is between dollars and cents; for example, $2.50 is "two dollars *and* fifty cents."

Special Usage and Style Problems

Parallelism

When several items are expressed together, they should all be expressed in the same way.

The class read, studied, and is playing ball.

In this example, two of the verbs end in "ed," and one is an "ing" verb.

All of these verbs should be expressed in a similar form:

The class read, studied, and played ball.

The class is reading, studying, and playing ball.

Parentheses

Parentheses are primarily used to include information in a sentence when it is important enough to be included, but not intended to be the main part of the sentence. They should be used sparingly.

That issue of the magazine (Fall, 1999) is a collector's item.

The sentence punctuation comes after the closing parenthesis unless the parentheses enclose a whole sentence:

I have investigated various photocopiers (see attached report) and have chosen one that can do what we need.

Please submit your records to the secretary (I have already submitted mine.).

Preposition problems

Be sure to use the proper prepositions in speaking and writing.

The paper was discarded on accident. (The word "on" should be "by.")

Use only one preposition at a time. Using too many can result in wordiness.

He took their name off of the sign. (The word "of" is not needed.)

It is acceptable to end a sentence with a preposition when to avoid doing so would sound forced or unnatural. An example is Winston Churchill's "This is the sort of pedantry up with which I will not put."

Special Usage and Style Problems

Pronoun misuse

I / me / myself. Many people are confused when they have to decide whether to use *I* or *me*. These are easy to choose when we have simple sentences like *"I went to the store,"* and *"Give the book to me."* In a sentence where a choice must be made, as in *"Bob and (I, me) went to the store,"* just try reading the sentence without the other person's name: "I went to the store." Since *I* is the choice, the sentence will now read *"Bob and I went to the store."* When you have to choose *I* or *me* as an object, do the same thing: *"Give the book to John and (I, me)."* Without the other person's name *(Give the book to me)*, the choice is easily *me*, so the sentence becomes *"Give the book to John and me." Myself* should only be used when *I* has been used earlier in the same sentence: *"I am not fond of sports myself."* A common misuse is "The award was presented to John, David, and myself." This should simply be "me."

> **"I have often wanted to drown my troubles, but I can't get my wife to go swimming."**
>
> Former President Jimmy Carter

He / she / him / her. When you need subject pronouns, use *he* or *she*: *"He directed traffic during the parade,"* or *"She knew the subject well."* When you need object pronouns, use *him* or *her*: *"The tickets are for James and (she, her)."* Read the sentence without the other name (*The tickets are for her)*, and the correct choice is obvious: *"The tickets are for James and her."*

We / us. *We* is a subject pronoun: *"We thought we knew his twin brother." Us* is used to receive action: *"This is for the Smiths and (we, us)."* Reading without the other name, *us* would be the correct choice, so *"This is for the Smiths and us."*

Who / whom. One of the most common language problems is whether to use *who* or *whom*. Take the "he/him" test to help decide: Look at the sentence in question, and in place of "who" or "whom," ask yourself whether you might use instead "he" or "him." *Charles was the man (who, whom) could get the job done*. If the answer is "he," you'll know that "who" is the correct choice. If the answer is "him," your answer is "whom." In this case, we could use "he": "He could get the job done." So the correct choice is "who": *Charles was the man who could get the job done.*

> **"If we do not succeed, then we run the risk of failure."**
>
> Former Vice President Dan Quayle

Quotation marks

Double quotation marks are used to present the exact words of someone being quoted.

"I bought the car today," said Mark.

They are also used to show unusual, slang, or coined phrases.

The reporter was asked to "kill" the story.

Periods and commas are placed within quotation marks.

You should read the opening lines of "To a Skylark."

I spent the morning reading "The Red Barn," which I enjoyed.

Colons and semicolons are placed outside quotation marks.

I was asked for my "address and phone number"; I do not know my new number yet.

If quoted matter ends with a question mark or exclamation point, these are placed inside quotation marks.

John asked, "When's dinner?"

But if it is the enclosing sentence which asks the question, then the question mark comes after the quotation marks:

What did she mean, John wondered, by asking "When can you come?"

Single quotation marks are used to indicate a quotation within a quotation.

Jill said, "She told me, 'I want to go along.' Those were her words."

For lengthy quotations, block quotations are used and no quotation marks are necessary.

Redundancies

There are many examples of *redundancies* that say twice what needs to be said only once, like "past history." Advertisers in particular use these to "hype" their products by using such phrases as "as an added bonus," "plan in advance," and "free gift." An extensive list of redundancies to avoid appears elsewhere in this book.

Sentence fragments

Unless sentences have a subject and verb, they are considered to be fragments.

I hope the numbers were incorrect. Very likely. Can't say.

These are common, and accepted, in verbal communication. In writing they should be avoided. However, they may be used effectively on a limited basis, such as to imply urgency.

Subject / Verb agreement

The subjects of sentences must agree with their verbs. When you have a singular subject, use a singular verb.

The <u>building</u> <u>sways</u> in heavy winds.

When the subject is plural, use a plural verb.

The <u>buildings</u> <u>sway</u> in heavy winds.

A good way to help you decide which verb to use is to imagine a shortage of the letter "s." Pretend that only your subject *or* verb can have the "s." There will be exceptions to this, but it will usually hold true.

When the subject is a group of things, it can be treated as a single unit.

The group was ready to go on stage.

Think of the group as "it" and choose the verb accordingly. But if the subject is the members of a group, the subject is plural, and a different verb should be used.

The members of the group were ready to go on stage.

Don't let the words "of the group" confuse you; the subject is "members."

> **"We are ready for any unforseen event that may or may not occur."**
>
> Former Vice President Al Gore

Top 10 Mistakes, Abuses, and Misuses

Top 10 Mistakes, Abuses, and Misuses

1. Using *it's* when you mean *its* or vice versa.

It's is a contraction meaning "it is" or "it has."

It's a shame about its broken leg.

Its is the possessive form of it.

The TV is broken. Its knob won't move.

2. Using an apostrophe ('s) to form the plural of a noun.

The plural of most nouns is created by simply adding *s* or *es*.

Snakes, skis, boxes, Joneses, 1950s, CD-ROMs

Apostrophes are usually only needed to show possession.

The snake's skin; The box's weight.

An exception is if an apostrophe is needed to distinguish between the word and the "s": *hair-do's* is much clearer than *hair-dos*.

3. Using the wrong pronoun for the job.

There is usually no problem in selecting *I* or *me* with simple subjects and objects. The problem occurs when these pronouns are used with another name.

We have been taught that when we mention another person's name with ours, we should mention theirs first as a courtesy. This is correct, but some people wrongly think the reference to themselves should naturally be *I*. This is not correct, because there are some times when "Mary and I" should be "Mary and me."

Suppose you have to choose in this sentence.

Come with Mary and (I, me) to the store.

Ask yourself which you'd use if Mary's name were not in the sentence, of course you would use *me*. So the correct wording should be

Come with Mary and me to the store.

Refer to the section entitled "Special Usage and Style Problems" for further help with this topic.

4. Mismatching pronouns and the words to which they refer (called their antecedents).

Pronouns should agree in number with the words to which they refer. If a pronoun refers to a singular subject, it should be singular.

*After the fire drill, each **child** returned to **his** seat.*

If a pronoun refers to a plural subject, it should be plural.

*After the fire drill, the **children** returned to **their** seats.*

Pronouns should also match the gender of their antecedents.

*Jane is clearly **her** own boss.*

*The boys took **their** equipment to the lockers.*

5. Using *who* and *whom* incorrectly.

Use *who* when you need a word to tell who is doing the action.

Who is going to the game?

Use *whom* when you need to tell who is receiving the action.

To whom were you talking?

6. Confusing *who's* and *whose*.

Who's is a contraction meaning "who is" or "who has."

Who's *going to the ball game?*

Whose is the possessive form of who.

Whose book was lost?

She looked at the fireman, whose hat was lopsided.

7. Confusing the words *affect* and *effect*.

Affect means "to have an influence on."

The speaker did not affect *my thinking at all.*

Affect also means "to put on a pretense."

She affected *a worldly manner to hide her shyness.*

Effect may be a verb that means "to cause to come into being."

You can effect *change by voting.*

Effect may also be a noun that refers to a result or outcome.

The effect *of the medication was immediate.*

6. Misusing quotation marks.

Quotation marks are used to indicate direct quotations; they are always used in pairs.

John said, "I will not be able to be at the meeting on Friday."

It is incorrect to use quotation marks to highlight words.

The professor was often referred to as a "stuffed shirt."

OR

Tomatoes "for sale."

No quotation marks are needed in these examples.

8. Misusing *lay* and *lie*.

Lay means to place something. It shows motion.

Please lay the paper on my desk.

Lie means to be at rest. It indicates a state of being.

She asked to lie down after she fainted.

9. Using redundancies.

We frequently use words together that actually say the same thing. We should be aware of these overlapping meanings, and only use one of the words. An extensive list of these may be found in the section entitled "Redundancies," but some common ones are "ATM machine" (the M stands for machine, so you're really saying machine twice), and "PIN number" (N stands for number).

10. Using incorrect verb tenses.

This usually happens because we fail to use helping verbs when needed. For example, "seen" is a good word to use in some sentences: "Have you seen Mary today?" But it is incorrect to say "I seen Mary today." "Seen" must be used with helping verbs like "have" or "had." Another word frequently misused is "done." It would be incorrect to say, "I done my work this morning." "Did" would be the correct verb: "I did my work this morning," or with a helping verb, "I had done my work earlier this morning."